MAHAN AND BAEKJE

MAHAN AND BAEKJE

The Complex Origins
of Korean Kingdoms

Rory Walsh

Published in the United States of America by
Michigan Publishing
Manufactured in the United States of America

DOI: http://doi.org/10.3998/mpub.11711726

ISBN 978-1-60785-579-8 (paper)
ISBN 978-1-60785-580-4 (e-book)
ISBN 978-1-60785-581-1 (open-access)

An imprint of Michigan Publishing, Maize Books serves the publishing needs of the University of Michigan community by making high-quality scholarship widely available in print and online. It represents a new model for authors seeking to share their work within and beyond the academy, offering streamlined selection, production, and distribution processes. Maize Books is intended as a complement to more formal modes of publication in a wide range of disciplinary areas.

http://www.maizebooks.org

Contents

Acknowledgments   vii

Chapter 1   Introduction   1

Chapter 2   The archaeology and history of Mahan
and Baekje   7

Chapter 3   The political economy of pottery   24

Chapter 4   Methods   43

Chapter 5   Mahan and Baekje sites   57

Chapter 6   Establishing core groups   75

Chapter 7   The social context of geochemical variation   87

Chapter 8   Discussion   106

Conclusion   114

References Cited   117

Acknowledgments

This book represents the momentary culmination of what I hope is a long and ever-evolving investigation into the ancient Korean past. What can be found here—and whatever is yet to come—owes a tremendous debt to my mentors, teammates, friends, and family.

This project was conceived and developed during my time as a graduate student at the University of Oregon, and I owe the very shape and substance of it to Gyoung-Ah Lee. The title of "advisor" does not do justice to everything she has taught me, from navigating difficult professional situations to the intricacies of Korean drinking games—sometimes at the same time. Madonna Moss has been a guide and inspiration from my first days in Condon Hall, generous with her intellect and always challenging me in exactly the right ways. Stephen Dueppen's relentless Socratic interrogations were the highlight of many weeks, and I sincerely hope they found a way to turn the heat up in his office. Daphne Gallagher gave me my very first authorship credit, invaluable advice on any number of topics, and a pair of the best light-touch forceps known to science. I spent many Winter terms in the teaching trenches with Frances White, whose pedagogy, collegiality, and leadership provide a model I can only hope to live up to.

Cho Daeyeon of Chunbuk National University and Leah Minc of Oregon State University have my immense gratitude for their assistance in my INAA research, Dr. Cho for recommending it in the first place and sharing his own experiences in Korean soil geochemistry, and Dr. Minc for helping me navigate the learning curve from my first cold call to the Radiation Center through to the analysis presented here. I have been privileged to enjoy the collaboration of a number of extraordinary scholars in Korea, including Shin Sookchung of the Hangang Institute of Cultural Heritage, Seong JeongYong of Chungbuk National University, Kwon Oh-Young of Seoul National University, and Lee Youngchul of Daehan Cultural Heritage Institute, all of whom have been generous with their time and their knowledge, as well as their archives. Jina Heo has been a big sister and a tremendous help, and together someday perhaps we will finally figure out who these Mahan people were. At a critical stage in this process, I am grateful for having been invited into the company of Jack Davey, Dennis Lee, Jonathan Best, Hari Blackmore, Marjorie Burge, Mark Byington, Lauren Glover, and Stella Xu, with whom I hope to rewrite narratives for years to come. To Rachel Lee, a friend, sounding board, and excellent travel companion, I look forward to exploring many more shipwrecks and bus stations with you as we work on our mystery novel and its many probable sequels. I will dearly miss the boundless generosity and community-mindedness of Martin Bale, whose advice both practical and profound continues to propel me forward.

My brothers in arms Habeom Kim and Hyunsoo Lee have my eternal thanks for their friendship and support, as well as for their frequent help with my linguistic limitations and logistical complications. I have at various stages in this project relied on the expertise, fellowship, and support of Rucha Chandvankar, Andrea Eller, Joe Henry, Jaime Kennedy, Maureece Levin, Angela Montague, Gennie Nguyen, Nicole Portley, Miriam Rigby, Evan Simons, Anna Sloan, Melissa Teoh, and many others in the University of Oregon community. The inestimable Rupa Pillai has my particular thanks, which would be true even if there were no book to show for it.

Since relocating to Ann Arbor to complete work on this book, I have been fortunate enough to find myself in the warm embrace of the Nam Center for Korean Studies. I cannot thank its director, Nojin Kwak, enough for making me part of this extraordinary team and providing me with a new benchmark for what a single human being is capable of. My dear new friends Hyewon Kim, Kate Klemm, Kelsey Langton, Do-Hee Morsman, Peggy Rudberg, and Evan Vowell have made this an unfathomably pleasant place to work, and Juhn Ahn, David Chung, Jaeeun Kim, Soyeon Kim, Se-Mi Oh, and Youngju Ryu have welcomed me with open arms. The University of Michigan is where I had the good fortune to meet Liz Berger, Andrea Blaser, Mike Galaty, Jim Moss, Kimi Swisher, and Howard Tsai, all of whom continue to foster my growth as an archaeologist and a person. Maize Books has provided me with a delightful experience for the publication of my first book, and I am beyond grateful for the support of Lauren Stachew and Sean Guynes, who took a chance on an unknown postdoc with an open-source dream.

My eternal gratitude goes to my parents, Bill and Ellen Walsh, for being my first inspirations and my fiercest advocates. My brothers, Ryan, Matt, and Evan, my sister-in-law Erin, and my young niece and nephew Gemma and Sam have been a constant source of strength. My dear friends Cat Crowder, Kate Ketcham, Kirsten Lewis, Lindsey Stafford, and Ryan Wallace have taken many phone calls and spent many hours on zoom, never failing to make me laugh when I need it most. To the family and friends who must go unnamed in the interest of wrapping this up, know that I appreciate you and will buy you a drink when I see you next.

This research was supported by the Korean Studies Promotion Service/Academy of Korean Studies, Ministry of Education of Korea (AKS-2015-Lab-2250001), the Korea Foundation Fellowship for Postdoctoral Research, the Core University Program for Korean Studies through the Ministry of Education of the Republic of Korea and Korean Studies Promotion Service of the Academy of Korean Studies (AKS-2016-OLU-2240001), the National Science Foundation EAPSI program, and the National Museum of Korea's Network

Fellowship. Support has also been provided by the University of Oregon Department of Anthropology, Center for Asian and Pacific Studies, Graduate School, Cheryl Harper Memorial Fellowship, and Edna English Trust, as well as the University of Michigan Nam Center for Korean Studies, Department of Anthropology, and Museum of Anthropological Archaeology.

1

INTRODUCTION

The archaeological study of state formation, so labeled, implies the result of the social processes at work: a state is formed, and a society is fundamentally changed. Our presentist perspective tends to assume the inevitability of this chain of events, that over time and particularly in the last two or three millennia, political structures will centralize, cities will grow, inequalities will increase, and power and/or authority will end up in the hands of a few persons at the top of the hierarchy. Archaeologists fight back at this paradigm despite the apparent truth in it, at least in terms of the long view. We do now live in a world populated mostly by people living in states, so clearly states have won the day over other types of social organization. And yet no modern state is without its detractors and, increasingly, a sense of inevitability in the opposite direction. People are making efforts to move "off the grid," to homestead, to prepare for apocalypses resulting from anything from political mismanagement to zombie outbreaks. While these responses to the state may seem extreme, they perhaps only serve to underscore that, for humans, life in a state is itself an extreme case no matter how commonplace this system of governance has become. The state and resistance to the state go hand in hand, and have since cities and civilizations began to dot the globe.

Resistance is easy enough to detect when it is happening around you, but finding evidence for resistance in the archaeological past is far trickier. Archaeology has a limited capacity to provide informa-tion on individuals or to tease apart everyday behaviors from ones that simply made a large impression—literally—in the remains of a site. As archaeologists, we can detect changes in cultures through time but do not always find clear evidence of what those chan-ges meant to the people involved. Did the shape of a tool change because it was being used for something different, or because diffe-rent people were making it? Or did the style of it simply drift with taste, fashion, or for no reason its makers could even name? Resis-tance is an ephemeral mindset that may result in certain patterns of behavior that are detectable, and in archaeology, little is more detectable than pottery. Making pottery, using pottery, exchan-ging pottery with neighbors near and far, selling pottery, buying pottery, receiving pottery as a gift, breaking pottery, and throwing it away are all behaviors that leave traces. Moreover, the patterns of these pottery-centric behaviors may take different forms in a society transitioning to state-level function and in a society that is resisting state formation. In this book, as will be outlined in detail in later chapters, the key concept in this differentiation is that of centralization. That is, a state economy may require the movement of pottery from the state's hinterlands to its center, or vice versa, whereas a nonstate economy would have no particular center, or many centers, all of which may move pottery among themselves. The lack of centralization will be indicative of a lack of state-level politics and, in the midst of many neighboring societies that are forming states, active resistance to state formation.

If centralization is to stand in for state formation, then the next question becomes how centralization itself can be detected in archaeological pottery. This ultimately requires a method that can determine whether pots have been moved from the places they were made, so the patterns of these movements can be identified as centralized or dispersed. For this, I have chosen Instrumental Neutron Activation Analysis, a method that returns precise quan-titative values for over thirty chemical elements, to provide geo-chemical signatures for a broad sample of pottery from my two focal societies, Mahan and Baekje. These chemical data allow for the identification of groups of pots that were likely produced in the same location or region, which in turn allows the interpretation of pottery transportation across various distances. I will demonstrate how these ancient Korean societies shed light on this critical question for archaeology and beyond: Why do people decide to form states?

MOVING KOREA OUT OF THE MIDDLE AND INTO THE CENTER

The archaeology of the Korean Peninsula has much to contribute to global understandings of how cultures have functioned and changed from the early Holocene to the historical period but has been woefully underrepresented in English-language literature. Often overlooked in favor of its near neighbors China and Japan, Korea is most often seen as an intermediary, its societies the result of interactions with these seemingly more vibrant cultural regions (Habu et al. 2008; Pai 2000). Such an approach reduces Korean archaeological cultures to reactive entities, and many chronologies of Korean prehistory stress the importance of migrations and cultural diffusions as the underlying cause of changes in the material record (Kim 2015). On the contrary, ancient Korean societies were dynamic, innovative, and complex in myriad ways, and while many did make use of their geographical position to manage exchange networks over sea and land, the influence of these was never unidirectional. Ancient Korea stands as an ideal example of indigeneity and external influence not as opposing forces, but as twinned processes negotiated locally in complex societies.

During the period of initial state formation in the Peninsula, the receptive view of Korea leads to the assumption that the Chinese Han Empire was crucial to why and how early Korean kingdoms came about (Barnes 2001; Rhee and Choi 1992). Chinese influence and even interference in Korean societies is undeniable, but in and of itself is not an explanation for the establishment of Goguryeo,

Baekje, Silla, and Gaya, four very different state and state-like societies active during the Peninsula's Three Kingdoms period. This study examines the kingdom of Baekje not from the view of its relationship with China, but rather its relationship with Mahan, the Proto-Three Kingdoms society that was both its immediate precursor in the northern Mahan/Baekje region and its southern neighbor for the centuries when Baekje's political apparatus was centered in the Han River valley. As with many epochal moments in Korea, Baekje is often seen as an external development, a prince and his retinue who moved to the Han River and began conquering Mahan polities (Best 2006). This narrative, based on historical documents compiled more than a millennium after the events they describe, has no support in archaeological evidence, and serves only to further undermine the agency and indigeneity of Korean societies. Mahan and Baekje, despite the overwhelming similarities in their material culture, continue to be discussed as distinct cultural trajectories. The current state of archaeological and historical research on Mahan and Baekje will be reviewed later in the following chapter, explicating the connections between these two cultures.

Studies of social change in the formation of kingdoms and other states tend to focus on elites, but understanding the function of such a society requires information from multiple internally defined groups. Chapter 3 discusses the concept of the state in archaeology, and how its importance is being challenged by theories on heterarchical power structures in complex societies. A common archaeological approach to social organization is political economy, and to this end this study examines Mahan and Baekje pottery, an artifact present in sites of all sizes and functions. Chapter 4 outlines a methodology using stylistic variation in concert with compositional analysis to investigate specialization, standardization, exchange, and consumption in the ceramic economies of Mahan and Baekje.

This study discusses ceramic samples gathered from nine sites, five associated with Mahan cultures and four with Baekje.

Chapter 5 summarizes the information from each of these, though in some cases this is far more robust than others. Three sites from the area around modern Gwangju City in South Jeolla Province were only recently excavated and only minimal contextual information is available, whereas the sites of Pungnap-toseong and Sansu-ri have undergone decades of research. The inclusion of South Jeolla material marks the first time this region has been included in compositional analysis, and reveals important patterns in ceramic production and consumption. These results are summarized in Chapter 6, and Chapter 7 identifies and tests chemical composition groups, establishing baselines for production signatures that can be carried forward into future work.

The ramifications of these results for the social, political, and economic function of Mahan and Baekje societies are explored in Chapter 8. Ultimately, this study finds that the production and consumption patterns of pottery in the Baekje kingdom bear a strong resemblance to those in Mahan, differing primarily in scale. Mahan communities of all sizes engaged in long-distance trade, and inhabitants of the larger Mahan settlement maintained relationships with nearby villages and towns in part by importing high-fired vessels from specialized producers in the vicinity. Similarly, Baekje elites in the fortified city of Pungnaptoseong imported much of their high-fired wares from specialists working at a distance, but within their political control. Long-distance trade was not as universal in Baekje settlements as in Mahan, but access to pottery from intersocietal exchange and domestic specialists remained available to people from a broad range of Baekje social categories.

The social processes that constitute a state or state-like society operate at scales ranging from the macroregional to the personal. Political alliances, economic developments, intersocietal interaction, identity construction, and social practices in Mahan and Baekje informed not only the function of these societies but also how we study them. A great deal of data on Mahan society comes from written records kept by Chinese scholars after travel to the peninsula had become commonplace due to the iron trade. Baekje kept its own records in the Chinese language, but all primary sources have been lost, and we are left only with later histories. Baekje's defeat near the end of the Three Kingdoms period led to the destruction of many records kept within the kingdom, and many Mahan and Baekje towns and villages remain underneath modern cities taking advantage of their strategic locations. Both the historical and archaeological records of Mahan and Baekje are incomplete, sometimes complementary, and often contradictory. This chapter outlines these issues, beginning with a broad view of the East Asian region and southwestern Korea's place in this interaction sphere in the first few centuries CE. After this introduction, the two oldest historical sources relating to Mahan and Baekje will be examined, followed by a detailed discussion of the state of archaeological research.

2

THE ARCHAEOLOGY AND HISTORY
OF MAHAN AND BAEKJE

Southwestern Korea, in a peninsula known for its picturesque forested mountain ranges, includes the greatest concentration of lowland plains anywhere between the Yalu River and Jeju Island. The region is situated at the nexus of multiple land and sea travel routes between East Asian geographical zones (Figure 2.1). The territory once occupied by Mahan and Baekje is therefore amenable to both agricultural endeavors and long-distance foot travel, as well as lying within easy sailing distance of the Shandong and Liaoning peninsulas of the Chinese mainland. Maritime travelers could also comfortably visit Jeju, Tsushima Island, Kyushu, and the rest of the Japanese archipelago from a home base in Mahan or Baekje. Travel between the southwestern and southeastern peninsula could be accomplished by both sea and land, via specific mountain passes that have been strategically maintained throughout history (Tsushida 2013).

From the beginning of the Korean Neolithic (ca. 8000 BCE), people on the peninsula had been incorporating new behaviors into their societies such as ceramic production, cultivation of domesticates, craft specialization, differentiated leadership, and long-distance trading (Bale and Ko 2006; Lee, G.-A. 2011). Trends toward social complexity were amplified by macroregional events starting in the late second century BCE (Byington 2013). China's Han dynasty had aggressively expanded its borders on the mainland,

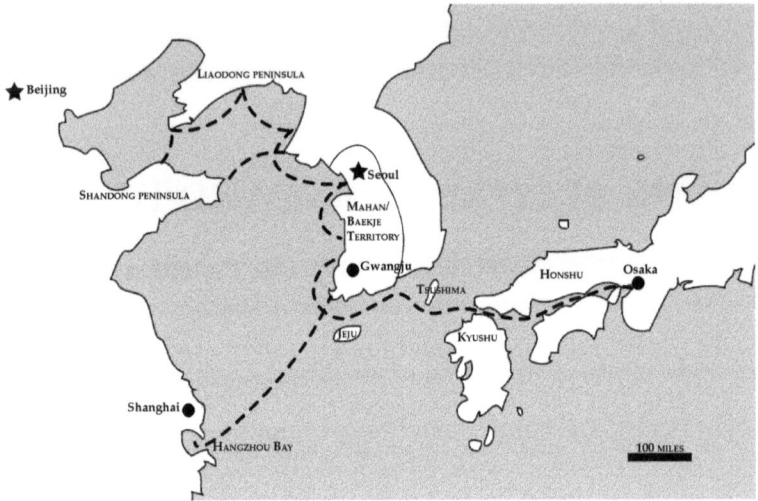

Figure 2.1 Map of likely sea routes connecting ancient Chinese, Korean, and Japanese cultures.

Source: Compiled with data from marinetraffic.com (2017).

and sought to establish a foothold that would allow it to control trade in the Korean Peninsula and Japanese archipelago. This was driven by the Han's desire for secure iron resources, and iron ingots became the *de facto* currency of interregional transactions (Yi 2009). In 108 BCE, the Han founded a type of mixed military/ civilian outpost known as a commandery named Lelang (*Naklang* in Korean, see Appendix A) at modern Pyongyang in North Korea (Figure 2.2) (Jung 2013).

Archaeological evidence of Lelang itself is available from excavations done by Japanese researchers during Japan's colonization of Korea in the early twentieth century. Though dating to the 1930s, this work on a 1,200 square meter walled site and a series of tombs in nearby hills yielded our best information on the daily lives of Lelang's inhabitants. The town appears well planned and organized, with brick-paved streets and a covered drainage system. Inscriptions on the roof tiles of one building identify it as the "Lelang Ceremonial Palace," the remains of which contained large amounts of Han coins and clay sealings (Barnes 2015).

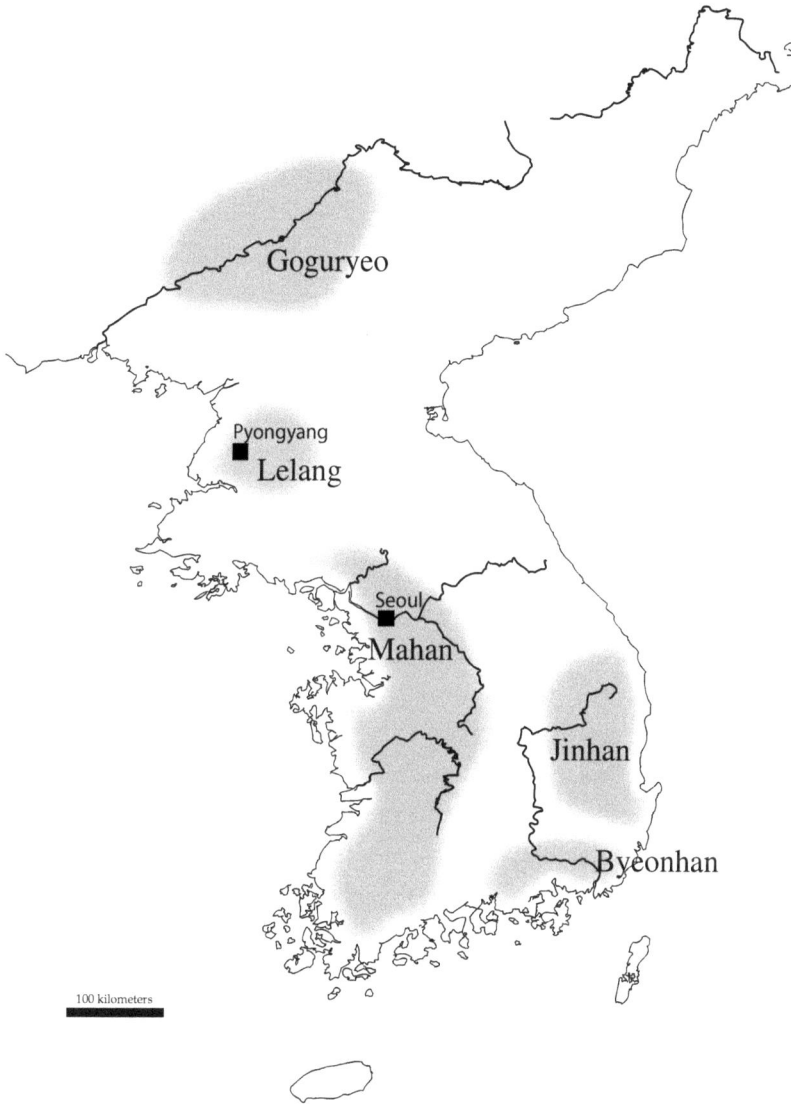

Figure 2.2 Selected cultures of the Korean peninsula ca. 200 CE.

Source: Adapted from Byington (2009).

Elite burials demonstrate that Lelang's leaders kept up with mainland styles, as the construction and layout of large tombs changes at a pace with the Han cultural core. Many of the goods from these tombs—bronze vessels, lacquerware, bolts of silk—were imported from the mainland. Korean-style bronze daggers, mirrors and horse trappings appear as well, indicating either the presence of Korean people among Lelang's elite, the adaptation of Chinese individuals to local culture, or both. Oh (2013) suggests that Lelang's wood-frame tombs from the first century BCE were built by and for members of the local elite who identified with pre-Lelang Korean society, whereas later log-frame tombs represent the emergence of a Lelang-specific identity, both Han and Korean while not completely one or the other.

The bulk of Lelang's population would certainly have consisted of Korean peoples. At the same time, the polity served as the nexus for trade and tribute between Han China and numerous societies in Korea and Japan (Lee S. S. 2013). A stash of Han-style mirrors found in Japan is often cited as an example of Lelang's reach, and commonly connected to historical accounts of the semi-mythical Queen Himiko (Kidder 2007). Long after its fall, Lelang's legacy was visible not only in technologies and craft styles but also in political organization, city planning, and the association of Chinese goods and ideas with prestige.

Lelang's influence and interactions with societies in the peninsula and archipelago not only were multifaceted and in many ways ephemeral but also had to occur along specific land and sea routes. South Korea is a mountainous country, making passage between arable land in the west, east, and south difficult. The south coast of the peninsula, however, is only 100 miles from the Japanese archipelago, with the large islands of Jeju and Tsushima available as way stations. On any journey from Japan or the iron-bearing mountains of eastern and southern Korea toward Lelang and on to mainland China, the likeliest route would cross or make a landing in southwestern Korea, the home of the Proto-Three Kingdoms Mahan society and, by the end of the third century CE, the Baekje kingdom (Lee 2009).

The descriptions of Mahan and Baekje in ancient texts not only offer many advantages to researchers but also create specific problems. Archaeologists may be tempted to fit their findings into the picture described in histories such as the *Sanguozhi* or *Samguk-sagi*, and may make assumptions based on these histories that would otherwise be decried as wild leaps of logic. As history was studied before archaeology was widely practiced, histories often take precedence in how both scholars and the public conceive of these societies. To address this problem, I will first discuss the historical data on the formation and function of Mahan and Baekje societies, and then detail what has actually been recovered from archaeological sites. The gaps within and between these narratives will present guiding questions for this research.

HISTORICAL RECORDS

Sanguozhi

The Chinese text *Sanguozhi* is positioned first for two reasons: (1) it was composed earlier than the *Samguk-sagi*, and (2) it describes Mahan, rather than Baekje, society. The *Sanguozhi* ("Record of the Three Kingdoms") was compiled in the third century as a history of the last few decades of the Han dynasty (206 BCE–220 CE) and the Chinese Three Kingdoms (220–280 CE), bearing no relation to the Korean Three Kingdoms. Along with the requisite imperial annals and biographies of notable figures, the document includes ethnographic accounts of China's neighbors, including Proto-Three Kingdoms Korea and Yayoi Japan (Best 2006). The text names the society occupying southwest Korea as the Mahan, one of the Samhan or three *Han*, an ethnic descriptor that still forms the name of South Korea (*Hanguk*, 韓國 in Chinese characters). While homophones in English and Korean, the *Han* (韓) meaning "Korea" is a separate word entirely from the Chinese Han (漢) ethnicity, which is also used as the name of the Han dynasty. Somewhat confusingly, it is this latter "Han" that gives Seoul's Han River its name, through a possible archaic meaning of "large." To the Chinese, the people living in South Korea were all seen as ethnically *Han* (Korean), but politically organized into three distinct groups. The other two are

Jinhan in the central east and Byeonhan in the south, which developed into the Silla kingdom and Gaya confederacy, respectively, by 300 CE (Barnes 2001).

According to textual analysis by Yi (2009), the *Sanguozhi* describes the *Han* as groups of allied polities. Each polity is referred to in the text as a 國 (pronounced *guk* in Korean), a word with the original meaning of "walled town," which has come to mean "country" or "nation" in the modern sense. The *Sanguozhi* states that each *guk* consisted of a capital town and its surrounding territory, led by a chief, but that one chief in each *Han* also served as political leader for the entire region. Based on these accounts, the Samhan balanced solidarity and independence on multiple scales, demonstrating a dispersed hierarchy of power and authority. Each *guk* maintained political and economic independence, and smaller towns within *guk* often had their own leaders whose power rivaled that of the chief. Some towns refused to ally themselves with any *guk* chief, and remained separate political entities. When military actions were called for, the towns in a *guk* would collaborate to provide personnel, and group identity was maintained by rituals that gathered people from various towns within the *guk*.

Some details in the *Sanguozhi* are particularly encouraging, such as the description of Mahan as the largest group, more than fifty *guk* to Jinhan and Byeonhan's twelve *guk* each, as this archaeological culture does indeed cover the largest territory. Most importantly, where the *Sanguozhi* provides the names of Mahan's many *guk*, the list includes one *guk* named Baekje.

Samguk-sagi

The second historical text of interest here, the twelfth-century Korean *Samguk-sagi* ("History of the Three Kingdoms," this time the Korean Three Kingdoms), was composed in Chinese by the Korean Goryeo[1] court. The *Samguk-sagi* presents Baekje as originating with a man named Onjo, the son of Jumong, the first king of Goguryeo (Best 2006). In so doing, the Goryeo court traced both Goguryeo's and Baekje's royal lines to the Buyeo "state" (*guk*, again, here with a meaning more akin to "kingdom") in the northern peninsula, from which Goguryeo claimed to have developed. From a historical standpoint, the chief problem with the *Samguk-sagi* account is the timing; Onjo is said to have founded the Baekje kingdom at the impossibly early date of 18 BCE, when Baekje was only in the nascent stages of formation as a Mahan *guk*. The text describes Baekje's expansion beyond the Han River area as only beginning with the reign of King Goi (234–286 CE), which more closely matches archaeological data.

References to Baekje's foreign origins are found in texts compiled both during and after the kingdom's existence, yet they are far from consistent (Ju 2009). Rhee (1992) suggests that Goguryeo may have invented a common lineage with its southern neighbor in order to foster goodwill, yet the *status quo* between Goguryeo and Baekje was warfare, not friendship. Certainly a young Baekje may have been interested in a narrative of descent to justify its kingship, but the motivation for a foreign origin is unclear. The historical accounts of the origin of Silla, for instance, establish symbolic authority without appeal to external justification (Nelson 1993: 243). One possibility for Baekje's preoccupation with Goguryeo would be the latter's closer and earlier ties to China. Baekje routinely deployed Sinicism to support its authority, in what Best has called "borrowed splendor" (1982: 446), and the story of the Goguryeo prince might be an extension of this.

Regardless of the origins of Baekje kingship, some decades after the initial expansion of King Goi, the Samguk-sagi has been interpreted to describe a quick and total annexation of the remaining southwestern territory by King Geunchogo (r. 346–375 CE) (Best 2006). In this narrative, by the end of the fourth century all remnants of previous cultures had been wholly subsumed into the centralized, bureaucratic Baekje state, even if this is belied by archaeological findings. This represents the height of the Hanseong Baekje period, named after the location of the capital in the Han River region, which lasted until 475 CE. (Debates on its beginning date will be addressed below.) The final hundred years of the

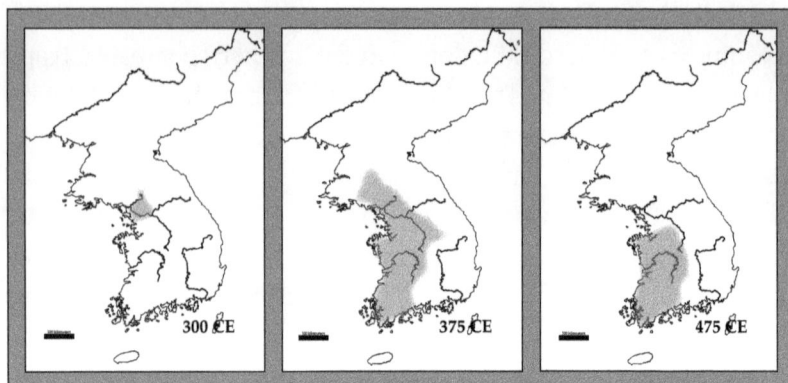

Figure 2.3 Map of the territory the Samguk-sagi suggests would have been under Baekje control at roughly 300 CE (right), 375 CE (center), and 475 CE (left).

Source: Adapted from Best (2006).

Hanseong period, if the Samguk-sagi's narrative is taken at face value, see Baekje at its territorial maximum, reaching from north of Seoul to the entire southwestern coast (Figure 2.3). Ongoing wars with Goguryeo put an end to the Hanseong period when the last Baekje stronghold at Seoul was sacked in 475 CE, and King Munju established a new capital at Ungjin. Despite the apparent subjugation of the southern territories, this move prompted a crisis among the aristocracy, as prominent Hanseong elites found themselves at odds with the leaders of powerful local clans. King Seong (r. 523–554) moved the capital further south to Sabi with the political support of that region's local elites, and proceeded to restructure the state's administration to regain centralized control (Best 2006). Sabi remained the capital through five further kings, until Baekje's ultimate defeat by Silla in 660 CE.

ARCHAEOLOGY

Transition from the Iron Age

The southern portion of the Korean Peninsula entered the Early Iron Age around 300 BCE, when evidence of processing iron ore occurs in the mountainous southeastern region (Nelson 1993). Unlike the preceding Bronze Age or subsequent Proto-Three King-doms, both of which involved multiple cultural traditions across the peninsular landscape, no clear sociopolitical divisions can be drawn for Early Iron Age society. This may be due only to paucity of evidence, as identifying the Iron Age has proven problematic (Choi 2008). Pottery, like much of the material culture, remained largely unchanged from Bronze Age forms and technologies. The most distinctive innovation is the use of clay band decorations, and the early appearance of footed bowls and ceramic steamers herald the changes associated with the Proto-Three Kingdoms. The two to three centuries that make up the Early Iron Age are therefore seen primarily as a time of transition.

Southwestern Korea contains the most arable land in the entire peninsula, but lacks the iron-rich mountains of the southeast. Yim (2014) has suggested that the southwest did not require iron due to its soft soil; farmers were instead able to prepare fields with wood-en tools. An overall sense of stagnation pervades the discussion of the Early Iron Age in the iron-less southwest, and yet by the end of this time the area had coalesced into the largest and perhaps most culturally complex society of the Proto-Three Kingdoms.

Detecting and defining a Mahan material culture

Due to the differential recovery of sites, the proto-Three King-doms Mahan society is known primarily through its burials. Mahan burials consist of a coffin, generally two large jars made to inter-lock at the rims or sometimes a wooden casket, overlaid with a mound of earth and/or stone (Lee N.-S. 2013). Members of the same clan were buried in proximity, and sometimes even together, as demonstrated by DNA testing on rare surviving human remains (Yim 2014). Variations in Mahan burial customs and other mate-rial culture have recently been seen as cause to doubt the existence of an overlying "Mahan" ethnicity or identity that lines up neatly with historical accounts (Blackmore 2019; Davey 2019; Davey and Lee 2019). In keeping with this, I will refer to Mahan cultures in the plural rather than the singular, keeping the historical name but not assuming uniformity.

The infrastructure of towns and territories described in the *Sanguozhi* is difficult to corroborate archaeologically, as relatively few settlements have so far been investigated. Presumably, the majority of Mahan towns were positioned advantageously enough that towns and cities still exist in these places and are thus obscured from our current view. This is especially true in the more densely populated northern region of the former Mahan territory, modern Seoul city and Gyeonggi and Chungcheong provinces. Far to the south in Jeolla province, Korea's "rice bowl," the relatively lower modern population has allowed for the discovery of over 150 sites so far (Kim S.-O. 2014). While further excavation, analysis, and dating are required to fully understand the settlement patterning of Mahan sites, Kim Seung-Og (2014) has complied existing data for a provisional classification. The vast majority of sites contain between one and one hundred houses, which Kim groups into small (one to twenty-four houses), medium (twenty-five to sixty-nine), and large (more than seventy). A few extra-large (1000+ houses) sites appear later in the local sequence. Larger settlements tend to contain smaller houses, and may include an internal division between large and small houses. Sites of all sizes have aboveground granary structures that are larger in correlation with settlement size. Kilns within settlements tend to occur in the largest and smallest sites. In large sites, these kilns are assumed to have produced wares for intrasite use, whereas kilns in very small settlements of two to five houses may have been used by more specialized producers.

During the Proto-Three Kingdoms period, ceramics from the Mahan region are utilitarian in nature, with forms including multipurpose short-necked jars, deep bowls, horn-handled steamers, and boiling pots. A frequent stylistic feature of pots from this region is the use of a decorated paddle to finish the clay surface, known as *tanalmun* (Figure 2.4). Two distinct types of tanalmun appear: impressions from a cord-wrapped paddle (*seungmun*) and a grid design carved into the paddle (*gyeokjamun*) (Tsushida 2013).

Figure 2.4 Examples of carved-grid tanalmun paddling decoration on a yeonjil vessel (sherd I15 from Incheon Jungsan-dong, left), and cord-wrapped tanalmun paddling decoration on a gyeongjil vessel (sherd L23 from Pungnap-toseong, right), shown with a 5-cm scale.

The same types of vessels used in daily life are found as burial offerings, and the ceramics themselves do not appear to have been used to mark social status (Choi 2008). The shape of these vessels, the horn-shaped handles, and tanalmun decorations make Mahan ceramics distinct from those in the southeast. The two *Han* cultures of the southeast, Jinhan and Byeonhan, are not as distinct from each other in material culture as they are from Mahan and, without the *Sanguozhi* narrative and later political developments, would likely not be considered separate archaeological cultures (Lee 2009). Pottery from this region lacks paddle decoration and includes a ware known as *wajil*, which was used exclusively in burial offerings.

While Mahan people did not apparently use ceramics to signify prestige in the Proto-Three Kingdoms period, other technologies do attest to social differentiation. Bronze artifacts become increasingly frequent in Proto-Three Kingdom sites, and include ritual objects such as bells, personal ornaments, mirrors of both Chinese and local Korean style, and weapons (Yi 2009).

Pungnap-toseong *and the rise of Baekje*

As interest in Baekje increased in Korea in the 1980s and 1990s, archaeologists began to search for the site of the capital on the Han River. Initially, researchers focused on Seokchon-dong cemetery, where several members of the Baekje royal family were interred, and Mongchon-toseong,[2] the last Baekje capital built in what is now Seoul, which Goguryeo sacked in 475 CE. A likely location for the earliest Hanseong capital city was not found, however, until large-scale excavations began at Pungnap in 1997 (Kwon 2008). Given the designation Pungnap-*toseong*, the compound was enclosed by earthen walls constructed in the late third century, estimated to have been 43 meters thick, 11 meters tall, and over 3.5 kilometers in circumference. This would have required control over a large labor force, and the organization of the site suggests an extensive central area for the conduct of elite rituals. Several large pits have been recovered in this area with the remains of thousands of pottery vessels, sacrificial cows and horses, small figurines, mica, apricot pits, and other signifiers of elite behavior.

The ceramics found at Pungnap and in other elite contexts include wares not previously seen in the region, as well as more utilitarian vessels. Two styles of Proto-Three Kingdoms pottery continued into the Baekje period: gray *yeonjil* (soft-fired earthenware) and reddish-brown *yeonjil*. The first evidence for firing temperatures above 1000°C come from the Three Kingdoms period, with bluish-gray *gyeongjil* (stoneware) and black "burnished" pottery appearing in Baekje. The development of blackware was likely influenced by Chinese porcelain traditions, as some designs appear similar to Yue and Western Jin styles (Choi 2008). Footed bowls, short neck jars, and broad-shouldered jars are common forms of blackware that do not appear to have Mahan roots (Seo 2014).

This new style of pottery, often called "Baekje style," has often been conceptualized as a prestige ware owing to its distinctive shapes and, in the case of blackware, its attractive sheen. For decades, the working assumption was that Baekje-style wares would have been distributed throughout the kingdom from the Baekje core (Nam 2013). This interpretation followed from the *Samguk-sagi* narrative of state formation, which not only conceived of Baekje as something separate from Mahan, its leaders foreign to the area, but also told of a sudden and thorough expansion of Baekje territorial control using primarily military means. This model of statehood supposes a powerful central authority, echoing that of Imperial China, elevated above the rest of the population to such an extent that even the production of certain kinds of pottery would be its exclusive purview. On the contrary, Cho (2006) demonstrated that the black pottery in question was in fact produced in various places throughout the Baekje region, using techniques modified from local traditions. The production locations for blackware were, however, fewer in number than those for plainer styles. Nam (2013) and colleagues (2020) point out that not only did various Mahan regions produce black or dark gray pottery predating Baekje blackware, but that when Baekje-style black jars were both imported and copied locally later in the sequence, these objects would have had different meanings outside of a central Baekje setting. This is borne out in the types of sites from which these jars are recovered. In Baekje core areas, blackware jars have been found in storage pits, houses, road works, and burials, but in Mahan cultural sites they are common only in burials. Some allowance must be made for the greater representations of burials in Mahan archaeological remains, but clearly these socially valued items tell us less about Baekje's political expansion than the complex relationship between various reaches of Mahan and Baekje.

Baekje produced a variety of other crafts and prestige goods, including bronze and iron tools and weapons, and a burgeoning gold industry. Gold and gilt-bronze adornments were an essential component of elite material culture, taking the form of shoes, diadems, crowns, earrings, sword hilts, horse fittings, and more (Barnes 2015).

Evidence of the Mahan/Baekje relationship
in Jeolla Province

Despite the narrative of conquest provided by the Samguk-sagi, excavations in Jeolla province over the past decade have demonstrated that a distinctly Mahan material culture thrived in the southern region through the fourth and fifth centuries (Kim S.-O. 2014; Lee N.-S. 2013; Park 2015; Seo 2014; Yang 2013; Yim 2014). Even after the Baekje capital was moved south for the first time, Mahan-style settlements, burials, and pottery persisted, with some incorporation of Baekje styles.

The Mahan has always been most easily recognized by its jar burials, which remain the standard mode of interment until the fifth century, during which they were gradually replaced by Baekje-style stone chamber tombs. As demonstrated by Yim (2014), even with this innovation in tomb material, the layout of burials in Jeolla province retained Mahan characteristics. Whereas Baekje people used stone chamber tombs for individuals, the Mahan mortuary culture often incorporated several lineage members in a single burial or in close proximity. During the fifth century and until the middle of the sixth century, stone chamber tombs in Jeolla often incorporated multiple individuals, and therefore cannot be considered fully Baekje-style. Some of these transitional Mahan tombs are larger than contemporary Baekje royal tombs, indicating the continued authority of local Mahan leadership. During the first half of the sixth century, however, tombs laid out for multiple burials tend to lack a primary burial in the center, even though space was left for one. This may indicate that while kinship groups remained important, the heads of Mahan clans were by this time discouraged or prevented from claiming a status that rivaled that of the Baekje elite.

With the number of settlements investigated in the Jeolla region, several scholars have made attempts to locate the Mahan *guk* as mentioned in the *Sanguozhi* (Kim S.-O. 2014; Lee D. H. 2013; Moon 2014). A political division may be evidenced by a gap in

Mahan settlements along the middle-upper reaches of the Yeong-san River during the third and fourth centuries. The environment is fully amenable to settlement, but may have been depopulated as a border region between potentially hostile polities. In the fifth century, a number of extra-large sites were established in this area, likely the result of Baekje settlers taking advantage of the open landscape, and not answerable to Mahan allegiances (Kim S.-O. 2014).

Kim Seung-Og (2014) suggests a three-tiered hierarchy for Mahan settlements, though the division between small, medium, and large sites appears more enforced than the result of a natural break in site sizes. Nevertheless, the difference in house size between small and large sites, and between different bounded sections of large sites, points to the reification of social hierarchy. The introduction of very large sites later in the Mahan sequence may be due to Baekje influence, as these sites existed side by side with similarly sized Baekje sites, but retained Mahan features such as above-ground granaries.

Iron products are less common in Jeolla's Mahan sites than in the north, and evidence of production is limited to finds of slag at two sites, Yeosu Wolsan-ri Hosan and Hwasun Yonggan-ri (Kim S.-O. 2014). Kim hypothesizes that iron was traded between *guk*s, whereas pottery production and exchange occurred internally to each polity. Indeed, a great deal of local variation is visible in the Yeongsan region's Mahan pottery (Seo 2014). In this region, the cord-wrapped paddle tanalmun decoration appears to predate the connection with Baekje, instead coming from nearby Gaya. In the fourth and fifth centuries, Mahan pottery incorporated Baekje forms such as pedestal bowls with lids, tripod vessels, and bottles, but in Yeongsan these were made with local construction and firing techniques. Still, Seo (2014) argues that Jeolla's Mahan *guk*s would not have been completely autonomous from Baekje, or there would be no social desire for such vessels.

The issue of the autonomy of Mahan societies and their changing relationships with Baekje during the fourth to sixth centuries has also been addressed with elite goods, largely recovered from high-status Mahan tombs. Yim (2014) notes that while over 200 Chinese porcelain vessels have been recovered from definitively Baekje sites, only two such items have been found in Yeongsan. Whatever elite culture existed in the region, it would appear to have been constructed differently from that of the Baekje core. Additionally, starting around the mid-fifth century, roughly the time of Baekje's defeat in Hanseong and southward relocation, Baekje-style gilt-bronze crowns begin to appear in Mahan burials. If such crowns were distributed to Mahan leaders, it seems unlikely that Baekje had managed to assert its authority over them, and rather presented them with such gifts to gain favor with their powerful (and now much nearer) neighbors.

With this information on the historical and archaeological record of Mahan and Baekje, the relationship between the two societies can be framed in terms of anthropological questions. Using pottery, an extremely common artifact in Mahan and Baekje sites, what can be learned about the ways craft products were made and distributed in these societies? If a basic understanding of the ceramic production economy in Mahan and Baekje can be formed, how similar and different were these systems? What can that comparison reveal about the lived reality of Mahan and Baekje people, how their societies functioned, and how they thought of themselves? The working hypotheses developed from the data outlined in this chapter are threefold: (1) Mahan culture persisted throughout the Hanseong Baekje period; (2) Baekje society had its roots in Mahan culture; and (3) both Mahan and Baekje people were active in regional trade and other relationships during the Hanseong Baekje period. In the next chapter, the means to test these hypotheses with ceramic data will be discussed, current debates in anthropological archaeology outlined, and the study of Mahan and Baekje positioned in global relevance.

NOTES

1 The Goryeo dynasty (918–1392 CE) took its name from one of the alternate forms of "Goguryeo," certainly in part to enforce their legitimacy in defeating the Unified Silla kingdom (668–918). Goryeo is also the source of the English name of Korea.

2 The term *toseong* refers to an earthen-walled fortress or city, as opposed to the more generic *seong*, a city.

3

THE POLITICAL ECONOMY
OF POTTERY

Ceramics are for the most part a fairly mundane class of artifacts, and may seem at first an unlikely candidate for decoding
ancient social systems. Many of us, however, possess collections of
ceramics in our own homes that speak volumes about the world in
which we live. A humble collection of coffee mugs may have origins
from points spanning the globe, whether due to personal travels,
social connections involving gift-giving, or an economy in which
household objects are frequently produced at a distance of thousands of miles. The very mundanity of these objects enables them
to record behaviors we don't think much about, but that nonethe-
less constitute the underlying structure of our lives. With this in
mind, we now turn to archaeological theories of the state and its
political economy, and how ceramics fit into this complex picture.

STATES AND SOCIAL COMPLEXITY

Archaeologists may use the word "state" in a loose, know-it-
when-I-see-it fashion, in terms of very strict criteria, or anywhere
in between. What an archaeologist means by "state" and why the
label matters is informed by decades of debates within the field.
The topic was pioneered by Fried (1967), Service (1971), and others,
who created explicitly unilineal evolutionary models of social development that end, inevitably, in the formation of states. In recent

decades, many scholars have tried to undo these reductive classification systems. The stages prior to state, most famously Service's
band, tribe, and chiefdom, have largely been reconsidered, but the
state remains an important comparative category (Shelach and
Jaffe 2014).

Elements common to both Fried's and Service's models of the
state include stratification (i.e., the separation of social classes
based on factors beyond age and gender), centralized leadership,
and some degree of force. Fried argued that a state is defined by its
institutions, both formal and informal, that maintain the stratified
structure of society. By the literal force of a military body, as well
as the fashioning a specific identity, the state maintains order "by
both physical and ideological means" (Fried 1967: 235). In Service's
(1971: 166–67) view, a state is built upon "bureaucratic governance
by legal force," whereas nonstate societies can be administered
with little more than an "air of confidence." These definitions were
fashioned from extensive cross-cultural comparison, and though
the works are clearly products of their time, they continue to have a
profound effect on the concept of the state in archaeology.

Subsequent attempts to define state-level society have tended
to augment Fried's and Service's models, rather than refute them.
Flannery's influential 1972 paper elaborated on the ramifications
of the band-tribe-chiefdom-state model for archaeology, emphasi-
zing the various hierarchies that develop in chiefdoms and states.
Feinman and Marcus (1998) saw Service's categories as a useful
starting point for comparative discussion, but also added to the
state the ability to draft soldiers, wage war, and hold conquered
territories. Interestingly, they also attributed to the state the power
to control information, an important insight into the hegemonic
authority wielded by the ruler of early states, and one only hinted at
in Service's model. For Wright and Johnson (1975: 267), the key element to a state was that of control, and most salient feature was the
presence of at least three levels of "decision-making hierarchy."
Working in the Mesopotamian contexts of southwestern Iran,
they sought evidence of this hierarchy in written records, but also

in settlement hierarchy. Crumley (1976) similarly viewed location and settlement systems as essential to understanding state power, not just over people but also over the land itself.

Another important aspect of state-level function is that of economic specialization, a concept intertwined with the differentiation of social classes. In Feinman and Marcus's scheme, only two social strata were required of a state, "a professional ruling class and a commoner class," though internal specialization was considered essential within these larger categories (1998: 4). Zeder (1991) saw the process of becoming and being a state as the interplay of a specialized economy, social stratification, and a centralized government. The production of specific goods by members of designated social groups is a particularly useful measure for archaeologists, as specialization of this kind is generally simpler to accumulate evidence for than ideological force or information control. As will be discussed later in this chapter, these more ephemeral aspects of statecraft can even be reified in the economic products that result from specialization.

Economic specialization, however, is not limited to state-level societies, nor is social differentiation, or even centralization. All of these contribute to the larger concept of social complexity, a term often used as a comparative bridge between states and nonstates. This terminology deftly eliminates the need to label a society according to a rank in an evolutionary model, and in so doing lessens the sense of inevitability of state formation. A particular problem has been a focus on "chiefdoms" as a necessary precursor to the state; Earle's (1991: xi) classic edited volume on chiefdoms referred to them in the first line of the preface as "intermediate societies." This theme was carried throughout several of the volume's papers (Gilman 1991; Kirch 1991; Kristiansen 1991), though some authors were careful to note the variety of social systems that can be lumped together under the term (Drennan 1991; Ferguson 1991; Steponaitis 1991). Drennan in particular refused to engage with the issue of whether the societies he discussed might better be called tribes or states, foreshadowing decades of classificatory angst (1991: 264).

In his lengthy attack on the use of the chiefdom concept in archaeology, Pauketat (2007) pointed out that the energy spent by modern scholars to determine the chiefdom- or state-level status of any given society is wholly external to the society itself, whose members certainly never wondered such a thing.

The evolutionary models that prioritize chiefdoms as precursors also enforce a distinction between primary and secondary states. Primary states, or what Fried (1967) tellingly called "pristine states," are those whose path from nonstate to state was not influenced by contact with other state-level societies. These states develop autochthonously from the nonstates—stratified societies or chiefdoms—that directly preceded them. Feinman and Marcus (1998) relaxed the pristine model in favor of the archaic state, which should be early for its region but need not be pristine, in order to expand the comparative category. The creation of such exclusive tiers within the state only serves to further sideline the discussion of secondary states, which are understood to have had interactions with other state-level societies from their beginnings. A primary, pristine, or archaic state is defined not only in contrast to its predecessors but also its descendants, and indeed any later state in a vaguely nearby region that would have been aware of that early state's existence. While the roots of a primary state, and therefore its hypothetically chiefdom-level forerunner, are consistently brought into the discussion of state formation, the process by which later societies in the region became states has not been the subject of nearly as much debate. The theoretical tautology of this omission was raised by Parkinson and Galaty (2007), who pointed out that the label of "secondary," once applied to a state, is often considered its own explanation.

The emphasis Fried placed on autochthonous development betrayed much of the reason for this imbalance: secondary states have generally been considered derivative in their statecraft, disconnected from the societies the came before them. East and Central Asia have proven particularly fruitful regions for demonstrating the absurdity of this assumption, with multiple studies in recent years explicating the complex and varied nature of state formation in and around the primary Chinese center. Shelach and Pines (2006) discussed the dynamics of identity in the state of Qin as it positioned itself as an imperial power, incorporating central Chinese symbols of authority while maintaining its own organization systems. Yao's (2010, 2012) work in southwest China has explored the intersection of state formation and function, identity, and material culture, particularly with the Dian Kingdom and its ties to various contemporaneous societies. The Inner Asian steppe has seen a great deal of attention as a location for decentralized, nomadic states (Frachetti 2012; Honeychurch 2013, 2014; Rogers 2007). Rhee et al. (2007) examined the ways in which Japanese societies adopted technologies through contact with the Korean Peninsula in the course of state formation. The work of these scholars clarifies the obvious, that there is no social development, no complexity, and no state that is not the result of local processes. Each archaeological state must be explained on its own terms, making the distinction between primary and secondary of little importance. If such internal classifications are essentially meaningless to the concept of state, the state itself as a comparative category must also be reassessed.

As noted above, states are considered societies with a high level of social complexity, but a shift in focus away from classification systems has great advantages for the conceptualization of complexity itself. Flannery (1972) defined complexity in terms of "segregation" and "centralization," directly echoing the dichotomy of state and nonstate social systems. A movement away from complexity as inequality has been led by Crumley (1995, 2005, 2007), enabling its use as an explanatory mechanism in a broader range of societies. Crumley (2007: 31) found some inspiration in the natural sciences when defining complex systems as "open, dynamic, neither completely deterministic nor completely random, and not in equilibrium," following the changing understandings of systems that have occurred in biology and other fields. As archaeology is a historical science, Crumley added that such systems undergo changes both fast and slow, and some of these changes have permanent ramifications for the system's organic and inorganic elements. The components of a complex system can vary in size, and the relative complexity of a system is generally greater as more components are present and interacting. Knowledge of the hierarchical structures of such a system is insufficient to understand its function, and Crumley argued for the study of heterarchical systems not only in cases where hierarchies are weaker or absent, but in all human societies.

Wynne-Jones and Kohring (2007) identified a strength of this approach to complexity in its ability to address social processes operating on multiple scales, from overarching political organization down to the level of the individual. This flexibility makes the framework useful relative to more rigid categorization that seeks to typify, rather than explore variations in societies. The concept of complexity as the combination of heterarchy and hierarchy has been successfully applied to many Old World societies. In Europe, Levy (1995) used heterarchy to integrate household practices, gender relations, and ritual activities into considerations of the social organization of Bronze Age Denmark, and Kohring et al. (2007) found evidence of communal sharing of technical knowledge of pottery production that challenged traditional models of chiefdom development in Copper Age Spain. In Africa, McIntosh (1999) demonstrated the complex social organization of large nucleated polities at Jenné-jeno in Mali despite a lack of apparent centralization or stratification, and Dueppen (2012) examined the ways Iron Age inhabitants of Burkina Faso institutionalized equality in a complex egalitarian society.

In an Asian context, Zagarell (1995) explored the coexistence of egalitarian and state-like social practices in first millennium CE societies in southern India, including the continuation of community property amid the emergence of wealth differences, and community autonomy alongside taxation by state entities. White (1995) argued for a reexamination of the model of Southeast Asian political development, eschewing the chiefdom-to-state approach for one that incorporates horizontal differentiation and social pluralism. Following this, O'Reilly (2000) showed that heterarchical structures in Thailand's Bronze Age societies help explain why urbanism did not develop with the adoption of bronze technologies. In the Eurasian steppe, Sneath (2007) found evidence for decentralized stratification in the aristocracies of nomadic states in Inner Asia. The focus on nonhierarchical structures in these studies has allowed new interpretations of social function and more rigorous explorations of political variation than possible in strict classificatory approaches.

Heterarchical theory has also expanded the possibilities for interpreting the negotiation of power and authority in past societies, including the construction of legitimacy for elite rule. As Baines and Yoffee (2000) discussed, societies require order, an underlying social organization, and legitimacy is the means by which the inhabitants of a society give permission for and are involved in the maintenance of this order. Elites often invoke connections with remote entities both mundane and divine to justify their privileged position in this order, which are materialized in goods traded in from exotic locations as well as city walls, roads, ritual objects, personal adornments, and other locally produced goods (Helms 1993). Though made by nonelites, such objects represent the efforts of elites to bring the immediate world into accordance with the cosmic order to which they have particular access. Materializing elite connections in this way serves to institutionalize them, turning ideological authority into concrete control over resources and their distribution (DeMarrais et al. 1996; Vaughn 2006). Recent work by a number of scholars has reexamined these processes by shifting the focus for behavioral explanation to nonelites, with cooperation emerging as a crucial component of increasing social complexity (Blanton and Fargher 2008, 2016; Carballo and Feinman 2016). Though elites use authority to consolidate power and control, nonelite members of society retain at least some level of power no matter their place in the hierarchical or heterarchical order, and with it the ability to resist elite authority (McIntosh

1999). Dispersed power is also materialized in the archaeological record through architecture (Blanton and Fargher 2011; DeMarrais 2007; Kristiansen 2007; Monroe 2010), trade goods (Monroe 2013), ceramics (Dueppen 2015; Kohring et al. 2007; Wynne-Jones 2007), and more. Craft goods provide an ideal lens through which to study these complex relationships, as production, exchange, and use patterns encode socially relevant identities and connections on multiple scales.

ANCIENT ECONOMIES

Just as classic models of the state are rooted in the concept of social complexity as inequality, most typologies of economic specialization assume a level of hierarchy is inherent in such a system. With that caveat, some important frameworks for understanding the nature of economic specialization have been produced that deserve a detailed review.

In an effort to codify the nomenclature of economic specialization, Brumfiel and Earle (1987) set out several key distinctions. First, several models were presented: the commercial model, in which economic growth occurs spontaneously in tandem with increases in specialization and exchange; the adaptationist model, in which political elites take a certain amount of control over the economy in order to make it more efficient and productive, whether for redistribution, market exchange, control of production, or long-distance trade; and the political model, where this control of the economy by elites is deployed in the interest of creating social inequalities that justify their authority through the creation of new institutions, monopolies, and wealth. In that vein, the authors made distinctions between subsistence goods and wealth, independent specialists and those attached to patrons, and staple and wealth finance. The difference between these categories may be arbitrary to some degree but can help reveal patterns in organization of production and consumption. Finally, the authors noted that elite control over the economy can be expected to be accompanied by elite control of symbols and ideologies, in materialized and recoverable ways.

One of the most influential pieces of scholarship on specialization in the archaeological record is Costin's (1991) classification system for the organization of craft production. Costin built on Brumfiel and Earle's earlier work but was particularly concerned that archaeologists were focusing on the exchange and consumption of craft goods, when craft production often has much clearer evidence and provides important information about social organization. To facilitate cross-cultural comparisons, Costin suggested a twofold scheme for describing specialized production systems: by degree and by type. Degree, in broadest terms, refers to the ratio of producers to consumers, with products made by a few individuals and used by a large number of people having a high degree of specialization. The type of specialization has more dimensions than the degree, and Costin reviewed the work of several researchers to arrive at four major categories. Each typological category was proposed as a continuum with two extremes, between which the reality of most past societies was expected to fall.

First, Costin used the context of production to describe the level to which production activities were affiliated with governments or patrons. Craftspeople can be fully independent, with no input from such individuals or institutions, or fully attached, requiring the sponsorship of these bodies to continue their work. Attached specialists work on command rather than as a response to market demand, and their crafts are more likely to include luxury and prestige goods rather than utilitarian items. Second, the concentration of production is a geographical measure, with a dispersed distribution of production locales on one end and nucleated locales on the other. A dispersed pattern has specialists serving every community, but a nucleated pattern sees specialists at one or few communities, and absent in the majority of settlements. Nucleation does not itself imply that the produced goods will not be available to members of all communities, but Costin pointed out that transportation may add to the cost or value of an item. Third, the scale of production refers to the relationships among the producers themselves, and how they are recruited to the craft. Production by an individual or a small kin group provides one extreme, with the other the wage labor system known in modern contexts. Scale therefore also incorporates the size of the group of craftspeople, treating it as a dependent variable with relatedness. Fourth, the intensity of production reflects the time devoted to the craft, whether it be part-time as a casual means to add to the productiveness of the household or full-time as a craftsperson's exclusive means of economic support. Some part-time craft production may be seasonal, engaged in when the demands of farming or some other work are not as pressing, or it may be one part of an individual's or household's normal routine. While these four types of specialization can theoretically exist in any permutation, certain factors are more likely to occur together, such as full-time intensity and an attached context, or a dispersed concentration and a small scale.

All of these parameters assist in the conceptualization of craft economies, but they carry sometimes explicit and otherwise implicit emphasis on elites as the drivers of economic change (DeMarrais 2007). Clark (1995) made an important critique by examining the concept of demand, which he felt Costin used as synonymous with consumption. Rather than invoking imagery from modern market economies, Clark (1995: 286) called for a focus on the "rights of alienation over goods," examining the various agents and motivations in the distribution of a product. Schortman and Urban (2004) addressed conceptual bias toward elites by adding to the categories put forth by Costin, Brumfiel, Earle, and other scholars. Four additional categories were included in production processes (Table 3.1), and variables in the exchange and use processes and political structures were added to provide a more holistic view of the relationship between craft and society.

This new scheme incorporates the issue of identity as it relates to craft production, which Costin (1998) had discussed in relation to her own suggested parameters. Not a simple matter of age, gender, or affiliation, Costin (1998: 8) recognized the identity

Table 3.1 Theoretical framework for craft production, reproduced from Schortman and Urban (2004: 188).

Variable	Continua of variation	
Manufacturing processes		
Raw material sources	Local	Foreign
Acquisition strategies	Simple, easily mastered, require little coordinated effort	Complex, hard to learn, need the coordinated work of many individuals
Production skills	Easily learned and used	Hard to learn, need considerable practice to maintain
Scale of production	Few people, limited steps, little energy investment	Numerous artisans, complexly organized production steps, major energy expenditures
Time devoted to craft production (intensity)	Part-time	Full-time
Physical setting (concentration)	Dispersed	Aggregated near elite compounds and administrative centers
Institutional setting (context)	Independent of elite control	Attached to, and supported by, elite patrons
Primary identity of the artisan	Not tied to craft production	As an artisan participating in a specific craft
Consumption and distribution processes		
Restrictions on the distribution and use of particular goods	None, decentralized	Significant, determined by elites

Variable	Continua of variation	
Demand	Low and intermittent	High and constant
Purposes to which goods are put	Daily maintenance chores	Political domination and resistance to same
Relation of producers and consumers	Equal	Unequal
Political structure and process		
Centralization	Power is diffused and situationally deployed	Power is con- centrated and institutionalized
Differentiation	Relatively few distinguishable identities	Numerous distinct identities
Inequality	Access to resources relatively open to all	Resources access restricted to peo- ple holding certain affiliations

construction of craft producers as essentially related to the "autonomy, control, power, privilege, and prestige" of their position in society. As Schortman and Urban argued, craft products possess value beyond the economic, and the identities of the people making them are not always defined in terms of their relationships to elites or each other, but rather are multiscalar and dynamic. Elites can engage in the consumption of craft goods without creating monopolies that result in dependence of craftspeople, who lose control over the exchange and consumption patterns of their produced goods. Inequality is one of many variables in this approach, and the authors remind us that goods that are used to enforce political domination can also be used to resist it.

By expanding the theoretical approach to economic specialization to include a greater sense of agency for the producers themselves, the question of how to recognize these trends in the archaeological record can be addressed more fully. Evidence for specialization can include the remains of craft activities, as with the lithic debitage in a subset of the houses recovered from the Korean Bronze Age settlement at Daepyeong-ri (Bale and Ko 2006), or by the presence of workshop-like structures, as will be seen in the kiln complex site of Sansu-ri in the present study (HUCM 2006). Most often, specialization must be interpreted from the craft goods themselves, and in these instances is closely related to standardization. A reduction of variety in vessel decoration, size, shape, and/or raw material can indicate a change in production strategies toward specialization along any of the axes discussed above (Underhill 2015). Roux (2003) conducted a cross-cultural ethnographic study measuring pottery vessels to determine the relationship between vessel size and economic specialization, finding that a higher degree of standardization generally corresponds to a higher rate of production. Roux warned, however, that emic concepts of standards can confound a purely quantitative etic approach. Archaeologists often have only limited access to complete vessels, but Hirshman et al. (2010) demonstrated that stylistic data from a sufficiently large collection of sherds can be analyzed quantitatively to address questions of standardization. Interestingly, the authors found that no reorganization of pottery production systems appeared to have occurred prior to or during the formation of the Mexican Tarascan state, showing that political complexity does not always correspond to shifts in craft economy. Standardization in ceramic pastes can also indicate specialization, but as Arnold (2000) has cautioned, social and geological factors affecting the availability of raw materials can interfere with such interpretations. In order to use geochemical patterning to address standardization, and thereby specialization and political economy, a full understanding of the choices made by potters during the production process is required.

CERAMICS AS SOCIAL OBJECTS

The study of material culture is essential to archaeology, but how to investigate past technologies with theoretical rigor has long been a major subject of debate. As outlined by Stark (1998), processualist theory marginalized the importance of technologies, seeing them as straightforwardly adaptive, functional parts of a social system. At the same time, sociologists in France were outlining theories of technique and technology that emphasized culture, rather than physical and environmental constraints, as the primary cause of variation in material culture (Dobres 1999; van der Leeuw 1993). Lemonnier (1992, 1993) was instrumental in introducing these theories to an English-speaking audience. His 1992 volume reviewed ethnographic evidence on various technologies, including the designs of modern airplanes, illustrating how the process of creating a piece of technology is rife with possible choices, some resulting in different outcomes and some not. Whether a craftsperson or aerospace engineer makes one decision or another, and how this affects the finished product, is based as much or more in what is considered appropriate as in what is most efficient or functional. Detecting these choices can allow the archaeologist to gain perspective on the social context of craft production, and track both change and continuity in past political economies.

These choices accumulate from the choice of raw material to the completion of the product, resulting in a "technological style" specific to the cultural context of the producer (Lechtman 1977). Style is a reification of behaviors patterned in particular ways because of how they are shaped by society, in ways both recognized and unrecognized by members of that society. In this way, the concept of style cannot be divorced from that of function, as style is present in every aspect of how an object is made (Chilton 1999). Rather, distinctions must be drawn among the various stages of production, and even further to distribution, use, and discard, as each of these is subject to its own variables. The chain of mutually contingent decisions that dictate technological style is known as the *chaine-operatoire*, or operational sequence, of craft production. Every action taken by the craftsperson is part of this *chaine-operatoire*, though only some of these actions will be apparent from the final product. For ceramic production, the *chaine-operatoire* includes at least ten stages with multiple options available within each (Table 3.2), but many will be largely invisible to archaeologists. The decision of where for how long to dry vessels prior to firing, for instance, can cause significant worry for the potter (Underhill 2003), but can only be observed archaeologically under very specific circumstances.

The problem, then, is to identify traits in any given collection of pottery that correspond to specific stages of the ceramic *chaine-operatoire* and to recognize how these traits encode the social context of the potter. Gosselain (1998) provided an excellent example through ethnographic work in southern Cameroon. (Gosselain himself later disavowed his ethnographic work in a piece (2016) that prompts scholars to be at the very least cautious with such research, but the example still proves illustrative.) Working with one hundred potters in twenty-one ethnic groups whose languages belong to either the broadly defined Bantu group or the Adamawa-Ubangi, Gosselain gathered information on *chaine-operatoire* through interviews and observations. The potters used a wide variety of strategies in their craft, including eight types of clay processing and fourteen different vessel formation methods. Clay processing, firing, and postfiring treatments proved to vary independently from ethnic affiliation, but Gosselain found a strong correlation between language group and the method used for vessel formation. The reason for this is crucial to the concept of a technological style; this was the portion of the learning process where new potters had the most in-depth, hands-on, and prolonged instruction from their teachers. The motions and gestures of the experienced potter were taught directly to the newcomer, most often a child or grandchild, until the method became inculcated as muscle memory. As knowledge of pottery manufacture was passed

Table 3.2 Stages in the pottery *chaine-operatoire*, summarized from Orton and Hughes (2013), Rice (2017), and Stark (1998).

Stage of chaine-operatoire	Examples
Raw material procurement	Finding, digging, and carrying clay; selecting and gathering temper; obtaining water; gathering fuel
Paste preparation	Removing large organic and inorganic inclusions; sieving; levigation; mixing clays; adding temper; adding water; wedging; kneading; trampling
Vessel formation	Coiling; slab building; pinching; drawing; concave or convex molding; wheel throwing; wheel smoothing; shaping by paddle and anvil; scraping; adding spouts, handles, and so forth.
Surface treatments	Burnishing; decorative paddling; stamping; rouletting; combing; incising; excising; applying clay decoration; applying a slip; painting; glazing
Drying	Outdoors; in the home; in a specialized building; adjusting time in different weather conditions
Firing	Open firing; pit kiln; updraft kiln; downdraft kiln; climbing kiln
Postfiring treatments	Applying various organic substances to exterior or interior of still-hot vessels
Distribution	Personal use; reciprocity; trade; sale from production locale; traveling sale; sale at market; sale by third party; distribution by institution or patron
Use	Cooking; storage; processing; serving and eating; ritual
Discard	Breakage and disposal as household refuse; disposal in a ritual process; deposition as grave good; interment as a burial jar

down through time, and the populations of certain ethnic groups moved through space, this particular stage in the *chaine-operatoire* was preserved due to the private and personal nature of its transmission. Being a relatively early stage in the creation of the pot, vessel formation is difficult to recreate simply by seeing a finished pot. This stands in direct contrast to stages like decoration, where established potters can easily adopt or adapt techniques they observe on pots with or without direct contact with the original producer (Gosselain 2000).

Compositional data, as used in this study, most directly address the first two stages of the *chaine-operatoire*, raw material procurement and paste preparation, with exchange and discard possible to infer when clay courses are successfully identified. As an operational stage, the procurement of clay is somewhat intermediate between conservative and malleable, with several variables at play. Clay is available in limited locations in a landscape, and different occurrences of clay can be of various quality. While it may seem prudent to assume that potters will use the highest-quality clay available within a reasonable distance, this is not necessarily borne out by ethnographic data. In a study on Kalinga potters in the Philippines, Stark et al. (2000) found that the clay source a potter used was highly contingent on personal relationships. Of 104 potters surveyed, most preferred to use clay from only one or two sources, but were aware of three or four. While the potters reported concerns with the inclusions present in certain clays that reduce the workability as well as the distance required to reach sources, politics also came into play. Potters in one community made use of clays present in terraced fields, and so each source was on land owned by an individual, who did not receive compensation for the clay mined. Landowners might restrict access to their clays at any time, and in one case in 1987, this was accompanied by the threat of a hefty fine for violating the proscription. Potters affected by this ban suspected the landowner was either trying to reduce competition for a potter friend or hoping to recruit the disenfranchised potters into agricultural labor. In this context, preference for clay

source was likely to be driven as much by the stability of a relationship with a landowner as with the quality of the clay. Indeed, preference for a specific clay source was not found to correlate with the
clay's plasticity, as was the case in a nearby community with a publi-
cly available clay source.

Choice in clay sources may tend toward the conservative due
to limitations of occurrence, quality, and proximity, but are also
malleable because of the social aspects of a landscape. Compositional analyses on the Kalinga pots gathered in the Stark et al. (2000)
study were capable of differentiating the two neighboring communities from each other, based on the geochemical signatures
of their distinct clay sources. Providing further perspective on the
social aspects affecting clay source choice, Michelaki et al. (2012,
2015), examined all the possible clay sources near a Neolithic site
to investigate not only which were used but also which were not.
They determined that a cultural concept of what constitutes an
appropriate source for pottery material was of paramount importance, with some high-quality clays available near coastlines igno-
red in favor of inland clays considered more socially acceptable to
the task.

Once identified, a ceramic compositional signal can then provide information on the movement of pots across landscapes. Minc
(2006, 2009) has used INAA compositional data to map the dynamic market economy of the Basin of Mexico, finding that subre-
gional exchange patterns persisted during integration into the
wider Aztec market economy. Stahl et al. (2008) found patterns
of change in ceramic composition over two millennia in western
Ghana that did not match the region's working chronology, making
straightforward explanations impossible. The authors suggested
that technological styles and exchange relationships were dynamic rather than directional, with some clay sources and consumption patterns fluctuating over time while others were maintained.
A large INAA project on pottery from the Iranian region found that
the composition of potters' tools did not match the geology of the
location in which they were found, indicating that Proto-Elamite

potters were highly mobile, traveling long distances to practice their craft (Alden and Minc 2016). A subset of this pottery from an Uruk colony in western Iran demonstrated that Uruk-style vessels were made with local clays, and that the colonists engaged in trade with local and nearby communities (Gopnik et al. 2016). In Cambodia, Grave et al. (2017) found that INAA was able to differentiate between products of different kilns where XRF could not, laying the groundwork for investigation into pottery consumption patterns in Khmer society.

Compositional analysis of ceramics can provide data on clay sourcing and past preparations, the first two major stages of pottery production. These sources are identifiable with various degrees of precision in different geological and cultural contexts, and can assist in understanding the nature of past ceramic economies. The degree of specialization observable in chemical and other traits of pottery has important ramifications for the organization of production in political economies. The social status of ceramic producers, their relationships with other economic specialists, their multiscalar identities, and the prestige of their craft can all be supported by evidence of the geochemical variation observed in pottery. The next chapter examines the methodological considerations necessary for the production of high-resolution data and appropriate interpretation of results.

4

METHODS

Ceramics encode a tremendous amount of social data, and archaeologists use a variety of techniques to extract and quantify those data. The primary method in this study is Instrumental Neutron Activation Analysis (INAA), and this chapter will explain the history and practice of INAA, while also taking an in-depth look into how geochemistry translates into archaeological knowledge. This involves considering what clay is chemically, what information the different chemical elements can provide, and what sort of mathematical models can be used to find patterns in the extensive data sets produced by INAA. Before the chapter closes, I will provide information on the stylistic analysis carried out on all samples in this study, as well as thin-section petrography used to check and enrich the interpretation of INAA data.

The assemblage of sherds in this study consists of three large samples from major Mahan and Baekje sites and several smaller samples from other sites in the Mahan/Baekje region. Since this is the first study to submit Korean ceramics to INAA at a facility in the United States, no previously compiled comparative database exists to facilitate the identification of local groups. The lower limit of sample size for the larger sherd collections was therefore set at thirty, based on previous studies where this was sufficient for the detection of relevant trends (Arnold 2000; Bishop and Blackman 2002; Stimmell et al. 1982). Sample size at other

Table 4.1 List of sites with alphanumeric sherd labels.

Site	Sherds collected for analysis
Gwangju Balsan	P01–P30
Gwangju Silye	Q01–Q15
Wonju Bangok-dong	J01–J14
Wonju Donhwa-ri	G01–G07
Incheon Wunbuk-dong	H01–H05
Sansu-ri	M01–M32
Pungnap-toseong	L01–L42
Incheon Jungsan-dong	I01–I23
Gwangju Hanam	N01–N10

sites was dictated primarily by the availability of sherds excavators were willing to submit to destructive analysis. The larger the number of sampled sherds, the more likely a sample is to represent the extent of variation present within a site (see Rice 2017: 317–27 and Orton and Hughes 2013: 48–50 for discussions on sampling from larger collections), so caution must be taken when interpreting results from sites with different sampling strategies. Some sites in this study are represented by only a few sherds and cannot speak to the full range of ceramic variation in the way a larger sample can. Upon collection, each sherd was given an alphanumeric designation starting with an arbitrarily assigned letter that represents its site of origin, followed by two digits, as summarized in Table 4.1.

INSTRUMENTAL NEUTRON ACTIVATION ANALYSIS

Ceramic provenance studies must take into account the geological and cultural context of their target area in order to develop an appropriate methodology. In some regions, stylistic and petrographic analyses are fully capable of providing meaningful results, while others require the use of higher-resolutions techniques such as X-ray diffraction analysis (XRD), X-ray fluorescence analysis (XRF, including the relatively inexpensive and transportable pXRF), inductively coupled plasma-mass spectrometry (ICP-MS, including the less destructive laser ablation LA-ICP-MS), and others too numerous and varied to mention. Each form of analysis has its strengths and drawbacks, whether in terms of the type of data produced, accessibility of equipment, cost, and so forth. INAA is among the oldest natural science techniques applied to archaeological materials, with studies beginning at Brookhaven National Laboratory in the 1950s, at the suggestion of Robert Oppenheimer (Sayre and Dodson 1957). In an effort largely coordinated by classical archaeologist Dorothy Burr Thompson, Brookhaven researchers Sayre and Dodson (1957) subjected a number of ceramic vessel and figurine fragments from known locations in the Mediterranean region to neutron bombardment, and recorded the decay curves of several isotopes. They detected what they referred to as "characteristic impurity patterns" (1957: 40), specifically ratios of manganese and sodium, that successfully differentiated pottery from different regions. Further experiments demonstrated the efficacy of the method, which gained traction not only because of the small sample size required to produce both precise and accurate quantitative results but also due to the appeal of nuclear science and expansive data sets in the heyday of processual archaeology (Bieber et al. 1976; Emeleus and Simpson 1960; Perlman and Asaro 1969). The laboratory methods and mathematical analyses deployed in INAA were refined and standardized in the 1970s and 1980s (Harbottle 1982), and archaeologists began to question the "self-interpreting" (Arnold et al. 1999: 61) nature of quantitative data, broadening their approaches to include ethnographic information and diverse anthropological theories (Arnold et al. 1991; Stark et al. 2000). INAA has persisted as a popular means of chemical characterization due to its reliability, and despite the closure of many research reactors in the United States. In fact, the limited facilities at which INAA can be conducted can be seen as an asset for building large comparative databases, as the equipment at each research reactor is regularly calibrated to ensure consistent results (e.g., Glascock et al. 2004).

The particle physics involved in INAA have been described in great detail elsewhere (Minc and Sterba 2017; Neff 2000; Pollard et al. 2017) and can be summarized as the irradiation of samples to cause them to emit gamma rays, which are then measured and analyzed to determine the elemental composition of the original sample. For this study, data on thirty elements relevant to soil geochemistry were returned, though as will be discussed below, only twenty-nine elements were used in most mathematical analyses. With large data sets such as those used in INAA comes the need to curate and analyze that data in ways appropriate to both the methodology and the anthropological questions posed.

GEOCHEMISTRY IN ARCHAEOLOGY

INAA returned composition data for thirty chemical elements on each of the 178 sherds in this study. Clay minerals are composed primarily of silica and oxygen, which are not measured here, but generally also contain aluminum, calcium, potassium, sodium, iron, and titanium on the scale of thousands to over a hundred thousand parts per million (Rice 2017). The remaining twenty-four elements tend to occur in smaller amounts, from hundreds of parts per million to barely detectable levels. While the bulk minerals generally speak to the nature of the geological environment in broad strokes, the twenty-four trace elements are crucial for provenance studies as their inclusion in clays is "effectively 'accidental'" (Glascock et al. 2004), that is, highly variable across landscapes and not subject to choice on the part of potters.

The inclusion of both bulk and trace elements causes some issues for analysis, as the data are at quite different scales. In multivariate analyses, many researchers convert the data to base 10 logarithms (Arnold et al. 1991; Glascock et al. 2004; Lindsay et al. 2008), reducing the orders of magnitude in the variation. Recent work by Baxter and Freestone (2006) and Michelaki and Hancock (2011) suggests that data that have been standardized, $((z=x-\mu / \sigma)$, or the value minus the mean divided by the standard deviation) better enable the detection of geochemical groups compared with log-transformed data. Following this, I have chosen to use the standardized data set for multivariate analyses.

The suite of elements returned by INAA contains minerals with specific relevance to determining geological provenance. These break down into five major groups, based loosely not only on metallic character but also on their relative contributions to clay soils, and tendency toward covariance. Discussing these groups briefly will assist in understanding the importance of geological context when interpreting INAA data.

The chemistry of clay

In order to possess the properties of clay, a soil must consist primarily of three molecules: silica (SiO_2), alumina (Al_2O_3, also called aluminum oxide), and water (H_2O) (Rice 2017). Water is added during the weathering process, when physical and chemical conditions in the environment cause changes to rock that transform it into soil. The silica and alumina are contributed by the rock itself, and especially feldspars, rock-forming minerals consisting primarily of SiO_2 and Al_2O_3. The types of feldspars present in a given rock will dictate a certain amount of the chemistry of the resulting clay, with other chemical input added during weathering, from organic contributions in the depositional environment, and while potters are processing clays. Three main types of rock are pertinent here (see Table 4.2): felsic igneous rock, mafic igneous rock, and argillaceous sedimentary rock. Igneous rocks are those that form directly from magma, with felsic rocks containing relatively higher quantities of silica, while mafic rocks have less silica. A typical felsic igneous rock is granite, and a typical magic igneous rock is basalt, both of which weather into clays under the right conditions. Sedimentary rocks form from material that has already weathered from igneous rocks (as well as organic materials), and are of

Table 4.2 Average abundance of trace elements in geological deposits, in ppm. Compiled from Kabata-Pendias and Mukherjee (2007).

	Mafic rocks (e.g., basalt)	Felsic rocks (e.g., granite)	Argillaceous sedimentary rocks
Sc	5–35	3–15	10–15
V	40–250	40–90	80–130
Cr	170–3400	10–50	80–120
Mn	850–2000	350–1200	400–850
Co	35–200	1–15	14–20
Zn	40–120	40–100	80–120
As	0.5–2.5	1–2.5	5–13
Sb	0.1–1	0.2–2	0.8–4
Rb	2–45	100–200	120–200
Cs	0.05–1.5	2–5	5–10
Ba	250–400	400–1200	500–800
La	2–70	30–150	30–90
Ce	4–60	80–250	3–90
Nd	2–30	18–80	18–35
Sm	0.1–1.7	6–11	5–7
Eu	0.01–4	1–2	1–2
Tb	0.1–1.2	1–2.5	0.9–1.1
Dy	0.05–7	5–8	4–6
Yb	0.1–3.5	3–4.5	2.2–4
Lu	0.1–0.6	0.5–1.2	0.2–0.7
Hf	1–4.8	4.5–5	2.8–6
Ta	0.5–2	2–4	0.8–1.7
Th	1–14	10–23	10–12
U	0.3–3	2.5–6	3–4

interest here because many are argillaceous, meaning they easily weather into clays. Sedimentary rocks can exhibit a variety of chemical characteristics, but some elements are particularly likely to accumulate in argillaceous sediments. (For detailed discussion of the molecular structure of clay and clay-forming minerals, see Pollard et al. 2017: 137–52.)

The thirty elements measured by INAA can be divided into two main groups, bulk and trace, depending on whether they tend to occur at levels greater than 1000 ppm (bulk) or less (trace). The twenty-four trace elements are further divided into four groups based on chemical character.

Bulk elements: Al, Ca, K, Na, Fe, Ti

Aluminum is the most abundant element in all samples here, often by an order of magnitude, since it is the only element among the requisite silica-alumina-water molecules that is measured by INAA. The next three bulk elements, potassium, sodium, and calcium, speak to the specific feldspars from which a clay deposit formed. The different types of feldspar are defined by the relative abundance of potassium, sodium, and calcium atoms that substitute for aluminum in the molecular structure of the oxides. Felsic rocks such as granites, which comprise much of the Korean Peninsula, are high in potassium- and sodium-rich feldspars, leading to potassium- and sodium-rich clays. Mafic rocks such as basalts, which are typical of volcanic landscapes such as Jeju Island, contain much higher quantities of calcium-rich feldspars.

The next two bulk elements, iron and titanium, also vary with geological environment. Iron, which makes up roughly 5 percent of the earth's crust (Kabata-Pendias and Mukherjee 2007: 210), occurs in greater abundance in basalts than in granites. This iron content is responsible for basalt's dark color and its tendency to become red or brown when weathered. Titanium makes up roughly 0.5 percent of the earth's crust and is strongly resistant to weathering, leading to its abundance in any clays derived from titanium-rich parent rock (Kabata-Pendias and Mukherjee 2007: 151).

As the majority of nonsilica content of pottery, the data on bulk elements are an important means of situating a sherd sample in its geological context. In broad strokes, a granitic environment should be immediately distinguishable from a basaltic one. While variation will always occur within a landscape, the bulk element data combined with knowledge of local geology provide the first step in identifying whether a sample has traveled from its place of origin.

Trace elements

Transition metals: Sc, V, Cr, Mn, Co, Zn

The elements considered in this study under the label "transition metals" are not, in fact, the only transition metals measured. Rather, they are the transition metals that occur in abundance of less than 1000 ppm, and have an atomic number not exceeding 30. (Heavy transition metals are included below under "heavy metals.") This includes scandium, vanadium, chromium, manganese, cobalt, and zinc. These are the lightest, atomically speaking, of the trace elements, those that occur in the samples discussed here at levels below 1000 ppm.

With the exception of zinc, all these transition metals are more abundant in mafic rocks than felsic rocks, with the distinction particularly sharp for chromium and cobalt (Kabata-Pendias and Mukherjee 2007). Scandium occurs in minerals primarily as a substitute for aluminum, iron, or titanium (ibid.: 127), and vanadium commonly occurs as part of iron hydroxides (ibid.: 161). Manganese, a member of the "iron family," often occurs as oxides that form concretions or nodules, which can result in a clay sample having extremely elevated manganese levels that may have little relevance for provenance studies (ibid.: 193).

Zinc is more evenly distributed between mafic and felsic rocks but is likelier to be concentrated in argillaceous sedimentary rocks, such as shale, which also weather into clays (ibid.: 283). While transition metals can be of use in determining geological origin in terms of mafic versus felsic, their abundance is also likely to vary widely within geologically similar environments.

Metalloids, alkali metals, and alkali earth metals: As, Sb, Rb, Cs, Ba

Arsenic and antimony are metalloids, elements with some qualities of metals and some qualities of nonmetals. The two behave very similarly and covariance should be expected (Kabata-Pendias and Mukherjee 2007: 381, 391). Rubidium is more abundant in felsic and argillaceous rocks, often substituting for potassium in silicates and also carried by micas (ibid.: 93). Cesium, another alkali metal, behaves similarly but with somewhat greater affinity for aluminosilicates (ibid.: 97). Barium in an alkali earth metal that can be precipitated as carbonates or sulfates, and tends to adsorb into clays as well as manganese nodules (ibid.: 119).

Lanthanides (rare earth elements or REEs): La, Ce, Nd, Sm, Eu, Tb, Dy, Yb, Lu

Of the fifteen total lanthanides, nine are measured by INAA in this study, and all behave essentially similarly. They tend to be more concentrated in felsic igneous rocks and argillaceous sedimentary rocks but can also be strongly influenced by organic contributions to clays (Kabata-Pendias and Mukherjee 2007: 133–34). This can make lanthanide abundance variable even from one clay deposit to another in confined landscape. The only lanthanide that is expected to behave slightly differently than the others is europium, which for unknown reasons exists in nature mostly in the +2 oxidation state, as opposed to the +3 of all other lanthanides (Pollard et al. 2017).

Heavy metals: Hf, Ta, Th, U

The heavy elements, as a group, are the least abundant in nature of any of the trace element groups. Two, hafnium and tantalum, are transition metals, while thorium and uranium are the two most abundant of the actinides. Hafnium can appear with minerals found in clays, such as biotite mica and pyroxenes (Kabata-Pendias and Mukherjee 2007: 158). Tantalum has been measured in highest concentrations in granites and occurs in minerals mainly as oxides (ibid.: 169). Thorium and uranium may substitute for lanthanides in minerals and generally behave similarly, though thorium also forms minerals of its own (ibid.: 141–42).

MODELING MULTIVARIATE DATA

Different mathematical approaches to the multivariate data set assist in revealing various patterns in the data. These can be applied to sherds as sorted by site or region, as well as to compositional groups identified by profile analysis. Each form of multivariate analysis has particular methods and goals, and its own strengths and weaknesses for addressing specific questions about the data. All of the multivariate analyses in this study were carried out in JMP 15 after the data set was standardized in R.

Cluster analysis is a tool for finding groups in data by looking for correlations across variables. Multiple mathematical techniques exist for computing cluster analysis, and as Baxter and Buck (2000) point out, the method chosen by any given researcher usually depends upon the defaults of the software package used. This study uses single-link hierarchical, or agglomerative, clustering, which first places each row into its own cluster and calculates the distance between each cluster (Livingstone 2009). The two closest clusters are then grouped, and this continues in steps until all rows form a single cluster. The results are expressed in a dendrogram, tracing the hierarchical order of clusters, and allowing the researcher to choose the appropriate cluster level for investigating specific relationships in the data. For instance, the earliest clusters of one and two are likely to be useful in a minority of cases, predominantly with outliers. The final cluster of all rows provides no new information, but the orders in between may show any number of salient relationships.

Principal components analysis (PCA) is another popular technique in archaeology, used for reducing the dimensions of a data set that contains an unwieldy number of variables. PCA plots the data into n-dimensional space and finds the line through the data that describe the greatest amount of variation. This line is the first principal component, and each data point is assigned a value based on its position along it. This process is repeated to find the axis of next greatest variance on the condition that this axis is orthogonal to the previous one, resulting in the second principal component, the third, and so on (Livingstone 2009). The numerical values of a principal component are therefore arbitrary, but any two can then be plotted in a bivariate chart, creating an accessible visual tool for understanding variation in the data set. Additionally, the researcher may obtain values for loading values on each variable, or how much each variable contributed to each principal component. These loadings should be considered when judging the usefulness of each principal component given what is understood about the variables in the data set. For example, in this project, neodymium was highly variable but unpredictably so, a side effect of the difficulty in spec-trographic precision for this element. If neodymium has one of the highest loading values in a given principal component, this com-ponent should be treated with skepticism. The first two principal components often account for over 50 percent of the variance in a data set (Baxter and Buck 2000), but higher-level components can be useful in teasing out specific relationships among samples. PCA can be a useful tool for finding groups in geochemical analyses, but the level of abstraction that results can cause difficulty for relia-bly identifying geological sources. Any conclusions apparent from PCA need to be verified with raw geochemical data and tested with other multivariate methods.

Once sherd samples have been assigned to groups, the mathematical appropriateness of each sherd's group mem-bership needs to be tested. A popular method of testing group membership is discriminant analysis, most commonly (in archaeology) linear discriminant analysis (LDA). Like PCA, this technique creates new parameters from a multivariate data set, but LDA canonicals—unlike PCA's principal components—are calculated for maximum separation of data groups defined at the outset (Baxter and Buck 2000). Additionally, where PCA utilizes the Euclidian distance among data points, LDA uses the Mahalanobis Distance (MD). An advantage of this approach is that the distance is absolute rather than relative, meaning that there is no assumption that a given sherd will fit into any of the defined groups. Once a group centroid has been established, the MD of new sherds from the centroid can be easily found, creating a useful reference in ongoing research. LDA provides a report on how many rows were misclassified in their original groups, and which group centroid they fall nearer to, as well as data on the loading of its canonicals.

STYLISTIC ANALYSIS

No analysis of ceramics is complete without an assessment of the pottery's visible characteristics and style. Prior to INAA, all sherds in this study were subjected to visual analysis to catalog several salient variables. First, their hardness was characterized as gyeongjil, yeonjil, or intermediate. Gyeongjil sherds are those of distinct stone-like hardness that reverberate slightly when tapped or dropped on a hard surface, often with a glass-like clink due to vitrification. The relative softness of yeonjil sherds is often observed as greater erosion, greater porosity, and a thudding sound when tapped. Some sherds display some gyeongjil qualities but these are not fully expressed, and such sherds are characterized as intermediate. Munsell colors were taken for the exterior, interior, and paste cross-section of each sherd. The exterior surface of each sherd was also examined for any extant decoration, including tanalmun paddling, use of a stamp or roulette, and slip. Sherd thickness was taken for both the thickest and thinnest point readily measurable on each sherd. Paste was examined for visible temper, and the degree of erosion was categorized on a scale from 0 (no erosion) to 5 (severe erosion) based on unassisted visual assessment. This provides an important baseline for assessing variation within the sample.

PETROGRAPHIC ANALYSIS

A subset of ten sherds each from three sites (Pungnap-toseong, Sansuli, and Gwangju Balsan) was subjected to petrographic analysis. Each sherd was vacuum-impregnated with resin to prevent breaking, mounted on a glass slide as a thick section, trimmed, and subsequently ground to 30 micrometer thickness and sealed with a cover slip. This standard thickness allows for the appropriate light refraction in comparison to petrographic reference samples.

Each thin section slide was analyzed in plane polarized and cross-polarized light. Plane polarized light vibrates along only one axis, and allows for observation of color and overall morphology of the thin section as well as pleochroism, refractive index, and cleavage of mineral inclusions (Reedy 2008). In cross-polarized light, the initial plane polarized light is reflected back through the sample at a right angle, enabling many other properties of minerals to become visible, such as birefringence, isotropism and anisotropism, extinction angle, and twinning. Feldspars, quartz, and micas can appear similar under plane polarized or reflected light but in cross-polarized light take on unique characteristics. Biotite mica, for instance, is highly birefringent, appearing in a range of bright colors in cross-polarized light, while quartz and feldspars remain relatively colorless. Feldspars exhibit notable twinning, or striations, along one or more axes of crystalline structure, and so become distinguishable from quartz.

Each of the thirty sherds subject to thin section petrography was characterized over several variables. The relative activity of the paste micromass was categorized as active, inactive, or intermediate, with careful attention paid so as not to mistake a highly birefringent micromass as active. Any surface treatments such as slips, stamping, or paddling were noted. The degree of overall paste density was described on a scale of 1 (least dense) to 5 (most dense). The size of vacuoles was noted on a scale of 1 (very small) to 5 (very large), generally with a range such as 1–3 or 2–5. Vacuole shape and distribution within the paste, as well as any evident paste mixing, were also noted. Inclusions were identified by substance and then ranked from 1 to 5 in density, size, sphericity, and roundness.

5

Mahan and Baekje sites

This study includes ceramic data from multiple sites in the Mahan/Baekje region (Figure 5.1), some of which have undergone repeated excavations for decades, and others recently discovered with only preliminary cultural information available. This chapter outlines the excavation history, known architecture and organization, ceramic assemblage, and geological setting for each site. When available, the contextual details of ceramic samples will be discussed in order to better understand how the specific samples collected represent the site as a whole. Details on the sampled sherds will be provided, including hardness, decoration, and, when possible, the type of vessel or object from which the sherd derived. Mahan sites are presented first, and the site with the largest ceramic sample first among these. Dating these sites is not always straightforward, as many excavators do not take radiocarbon dates on historical strata and therefore little comparative data exist to put the few available dates in context. All Mahan sites here appear to have been occupied during the second to fourth centuries CE, with Gwangju Balsan originating near the end of that period and continuing on to roughly the fifth century (Figure 5.2). The discussion of Baekje sites begins with a kiln complex, as this is expected to provide important context for the other sites in following chapters. Baekje sites then continue from largest ceramic sample to smallest. Last, geological information about all regions in this study will be provided.

Figure 5.1 Map showing locations of sites in this study.

MAHAN SITES

Balsan, Oseon-dong, Gwangju Metropolitan City (South Jeolla Province[1])

Modern Gwangju City, roughly 265 kilometers directly south of Seoul, is the largest city in the heavily agricultural province of

Mahan Sites

	1–100 CE	101–200 CE	201–300 CE	301–400 CE	401–500 CE	501–600 CE
Gwangju Oseon-dong (Balsan & Silye)						
Wonju Bangok-dong						
Wonju Donghwa-ri						
Incheon Wunbuk-dong						

Baekje Sites

Sansu-ri						
Pungnap-toseong						
Incheon Jungsan-dong						
Gwangju Hanam						

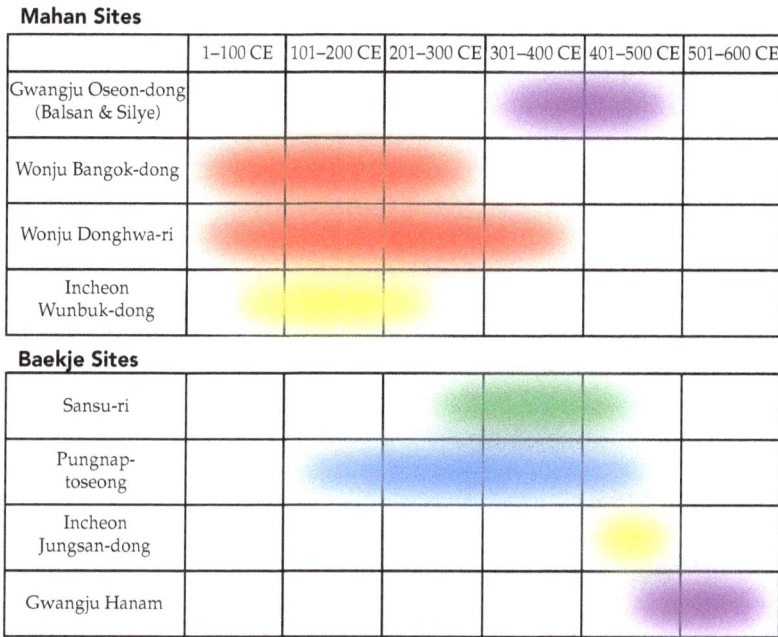

Figure 5.2 Chronology of the sites in this study, showing an approximate range of occupation.

South Jeolla. The Mahan site of Gwangju Balsan was uncovered in the neighborhood of Oseon-dong near the northwestern edge of the city in 2013, and a full site report is still being compiled. While AMS dates and a finalized list of features are not available, qualitative comparative dates on artifacts place the site's origins in the fourth century, roughly contemporaneous to the Hanseong Baekje period. Communication with the excavators indicates the site was very large for its time, with 190 pit houses identified so far, along with postholes laid out for thirty-nine aboveground buildings and two wells. The ceramic sample from Gwangju Balsan is comprised of thirty sherds from twenty-nine different house features. These sherds were collected with the goal of creating an approximately representative sample of Balsan ceramics.

The sample of thirty sherds from Gwangju Balsan is dominated by yeonjil sherds, with twenty-three in total. Three sherds are of gyeongjil hardness, and four are intermediate. The dominant form of decoration at Balsan is carved-grid tanalmun paddling (n = 15), and three sherds show some form of vertical line decoration. Sherds from Balsan are fragmentary and no vessel types could be determined in this portion of the sample.

Silye, Oseon-dong, Gwangju Metropolitan City (South Jeolla Province)

The excavation at Silye took place immediately south of Balsan; the two sites fit within a single square kilometer. Identified in the same survey project as Balsan, Silye was excavated one field season earlier, in 2012. Though only a preliminary report is available, the artifact styles have been used to date the site occupation from the fourth century to the mid-fifth century. The site contains 170 pit houses, 10 square buildings that do not appear to be residences, 60 aboveground structures, 5 mounded tombs, and even a 20 by 20 meter section of preserved agricultural field. Excavators noted that pit houses in Silye varied in size, with roughly 90 percent under 20 square meters, 7 percent between 20 and 30 square meters, and only 3 percent over 30 square meters. The fifteen sherds sampled from Silye all come from the mounded tombs, to provide a counterpoint with the domestic data from Balsan.

Twelve out of fifteen sherds at Silye are of gyeongjil hardness, with the remaining three intermediate. Five sherds show carved-grid tanalmun paddling, and five show carved-linear tanalmun paddling, with an additional sherd showing both paddled patterns. Two sherds have a stamped linear design, applied in a neater fashion than its paddled equivalents. Only two sherds are large enough to determine the vessel type, and both are jars.

Bangok-dong, Wonju City, Gangwon Province

The city of Wonju is located in the extreme southwest of Gangwon Province, approximately 75 kilometers southeast of Seoul. Wonju is the most populous city in Gangwon, lying almost precisely between the east and west coasts in an important mountain pass. For both Mahan and Baekje societies, the Wonju region would have represented the eastern extreme of influence. Bangok-dong (phonetically *ban-gok-dong*) is neighborhood on the east side of Wonju City, bordering on Chiaksan National Park to the east and the Wonju River on the west. Excavations at Bangok-dong commenced with plans to build the Innovation City Complex, and uncovered remains from the Neolithic, Bronze Age, Proto-Three Kingdoms, United Silla, and later periods.

Unfortunately, no AMS dates were taken from Proto-Three Kingdoms or later period features. The Mahan settlement, which is located near the river, consists of seventeen house remains and seven pit features (HICH 2013). Several of the houses overlap, and it is unclear how many were occupied simultaneously. All the houses face southeast, built roughly parallel to the river course. Most houses have at least a short entryway on their southeast sides, with some of these having been elaborated to anterooms, particularly in the houses furthest south, including 13, 16, and 17. Ceramic remains from houses include large storage jars, straight-necked jars, steamer pots, deep bowls, low bowls, and spindle whorls. A curious tripod cup with two small lug handles was excavated from House 17, its shape reminiscent of a crucible, standing 5.6 centimeters tall. Decorations on vessels includes cord-wrapped and carved paddling, occasionally with the addition of incised horizontal lines to provide a banded effect to the design, banded vertical lines, and incised cross-hatching. Ten sampled sherds come from house contexts, and six of these from House 16, an ante-chambered house with a central floor hearth similar to House 5 at Donghwa-ri, discussed below. Three sherds come from pit features, and one from surface collection.

Donghwa-ri, Munmak-eup, Wonju City, Gangwon Province

West of the city proper, in the administrative district of Munmak, the Wonju Donghwa-ri site was discovered during the construction of the Anchang Bridge across the Seom River, a tributary of the Han. In addition to small Bronze Age and historical components, five Proto-Three Kingdoms houses were excavated, along with twenty-three pit features (HICH 2008). The houses date between the second century and the fourth century based on pottery seriation, and AMS dates taken on wood charcoal returned results in the first two centuries CE. (See Appendix B for a table of all relevant AMS dates, though these are limited due to a tendency not to date historical and proto-historical sites.) Domestic architecture at Donghwa-ri is somewhat variable. House 1 is very long, roughly 4 meters across the front and extending back nearly 10 meters, with the back wall not found due to postdepositional disturbance. The front of House 1 curves into a short entryway, whereas a longer entryway with a small antechamber leads to the overall smaller House 2, which measures only about 4 by 4 meters square. Houses 3 and 4 are each roughly 5 by 6 meters, but have large portions missing from disturbance. While no entryways are apparent, it cannot be said with certainty that none existed. House 5 is extended into two rooms via a short passage from one 4 by 5 meter space into a 2 by 3 meter space. The hearth of House 5 is a simple floor hearth in the center of the larger room, but the other, less architecturally elaborate houses have stone-lined or raised cooktop hearths.

The ceramics recovered also vary across houses, with modest remains from Houses 1 and 2 including jars and bowls, and the remains from the less well-preserved Houses 3 and 4 including multiple large storage jars in addition to smaller jars and bowls. House 5 contains storage jars, smaller jars, and bowls, and also a higher concentration of tools such as ceramic spindle whorls and stone chisels than in other houses. Decoration on ceramics includes cord-wrapped and carved paddling, incised parallel lines, and circular and diamond-shaped impressions. The seven sherds included in this study all come from the house remains, but contextual data on which house are not available.

The twenty-one sherds from both sites at Wonju include no gyeongjil or gray wares, with two sherds of intermediate hardness and nineteen yeonjil. Decoration is somewhat less prevalent at Wonju than at other sites, but more varied. Six sherds are decorated, one with carved-grid tanalmun, two with cord-wrapped tanalmun, two with dragged combs, and one with incised horizontal lines. One sherd can be identified as a straight-necked jar, but the others are body sherds with no clear vessel type.

Wunbuk-dong, Yeongjong Island, Incheon Metropolitan City (Gyeonggi Province)

Modern Yeongjong Island was created by a land reclamation project that connected three other islands to Yeongjong for the purpose of constructing Incheon International Airport. The island lies 2 kilometers off the west coast among many smaller islands in the territory of Incheon City, and is now connected to the peninsula by two major bridges. The airport and much of its associated development occupy the reclaimed portions of the island, but new construction projects on the original Yeongjong Island have revealed the multicomponent sites of Wunbuk-dong and Jungsan-dong (discussed below). Wunbuk-dong was excavated in the northeast section of the island from 2008 to 2010, with the majority of features dating to the Neolithic.

Two houses and eight pit features date to the Proto-Three Kingdoms, confirmed both by AMS dating and the presence of Chinese *wuzhuqian* (五銖錢) coins produced between 2 BCE and 7 CE (HICH 2012b). The presence of fragments of Chinese scaled armor and Chinese ceramics suggests trade with the Lelang commandery. The excavators point out, however, that the coins and iron and bronze arrowheads also recovered were less likely to have been produced at Lelang, and may indicate trade with other Chinese regions.

Ceramics from the Proto-Three Kingdoms features include small pots and bowls of Chinese grayware, Korean attached-rim pottery, and storage jars of both Chinese and Korean manufacture. Five sherds were sampled from the two houses, all of which are too small to identify the shape or style of their constituent pots. The five sherds from Wunbuk-dong contain four yeonjil and one sherd of intermediate hardness, and none of the five show decoration, though that may be a factor of their small size.

BAEKJE SITES

Sansu-ri/Samryong-ri, Jincheon County, North Chungcheong Province

The remains of a large kiln complex active during the late Mahan and early Baekje periods straddle the modern boundary between the towns of Sansu-ri and Samryong-ri in Jincheon County, North Chungcheong Province. Excavations began in 1986, and the 1987 season revealed a cluster of seven kilns at Sansu-ri, inviting national attention and leading to the use of "Sansu-ri" as a shorthand name for the entire site. Twenty kilns, two areas identified as pottery workshops, and numerous dwellings were excavated between 1987 and 1992, and though the majority of material came from the Samryong-ri side, the site is still known primarily as Sansu-ri, as it will be referred to here. The chronology of Sansu-ri has been difficult to ascertain (Cho 2006), and most arguments revolve around the sequencing of ceramics that may have been contemporaneous (*in sensu* Kim J. S. 2014). The excavators proposed a five-period scheme based on pottery chronologies, correlating the passage of time with the increase of vessel forms (HUCM 2006). Although this has not yet been thoroughly tested with absolute dating techniques, stylistic analysis is sufficient to argue for a major phase of Sansu-ri's occupation and use placed in the Hanseong Baekje period, contemporaneous with the occupation of Pungnap-toseong (Cho 2006).

The kilns at Sansu-ri are of the type described by Cho (2006) as "cross-draft," long ovoid structures deliberately placed on the side of gently sloping hills. The firebox for each kiln was placed at the lowest elevation to allow heat to flow up into the pottery chamber.

Some kilns, such as Kilns 90–95, show evidence of remodeling over four or more phases of use (HUCM 2006). The kilns occur in three groups of six or seven each, separated from each other by distances of 100–500 meters. Houses occur in small numbers both near kilns and in areas without kilns. The scattered nature of the excavation units has thus far obscured the overall pattern of settlement at the site (ibid.).

The ceramic remains at Sansu-ri are dominated by jars, suggesting their specialized production by the potters at the site. A Sansu-ri jar is easy to recognize by its distinctive decoration in ranks of stamped vertical lines, forming horizontal bands across the body of the jar (Figure 5.3). Tanalmun decorations also appear in a minority of vessels, and impressions of anvils occur on the interior of vessels even when no decorative paddling was applied.

Figure 5.3 Examples of typical decoration on jars at Sansu-ri, showing horizontal bands of short vertical lines. Sherds pictured are M21 (left) and M18 (right) from the Sansu-ri sample in this study.

Some pottery-making tools have been recovered, including anvils, and experiments have reconstructed the stamps required to form the linear decorations. Ceramic forms recovered aside from the distinctive jars include cooking pots, bowls, deep bowls, and possible tools such as a tile with small round impressions, an 11.5-centimeter-long ceramic tube, and various perforated or semi-hollow objects of indeterminate function. These nonjar forms are more commonly found in dwellings and in the two reported workshop structures (HUCM 2006).

Sherd samples were collected from numerous contexts at Sansu-ri, including eighteen kilns and five houses excavated from 1987 to 1991. Although no samples were taken from complete vessels, many sherds are clearly from typical jars, and possess the banded linear incisions so prevalent at the site. The only sherd not from a vessel is a portion of ceramic piping from House 88–2. Of the thirty-two sherd samples collected, six come from house remains and twenty-six from cross-draft kilns. The balance is therefore weighted toward kilns, and any interpretations should account for the difference in behavioral implications between objects found in kilns and those excavated from household contexts.

The sherds in the sample from Sansu-ri are the most similar of any site, with twenty-three gyeongjil sherds, six yeonjil, and three intermediate. Twenty-four sherds are decorated, twenty-three with the distinctive stamped parallel lines that have been routinely used to identify Sansu-ri-made ceramics. The remaining decorated sherd has carved-grid tanalmun paddling. Four sherds are clearly from jars, the vessel most often associated with Sansu-ri production, two more possibly from storage jars, and three from bowls.

Pungnap-toseong, Pungnap-dong, Songpa District, Seoul Special City (Gyeonggi Province)

The discovery and significance of the earthen-walled fortress known as Pungnap-toseong were summarized in Chapter 2. The massive, 3.5-kilometer-long encircling wall of the site still encloses

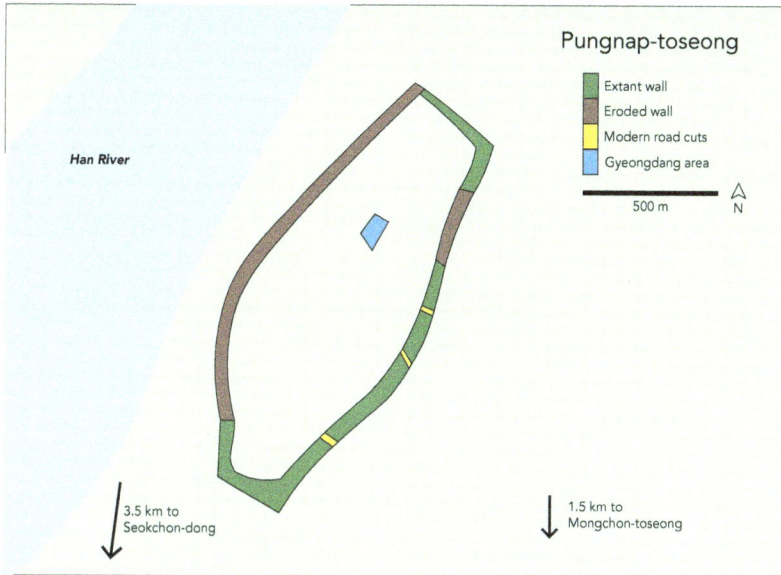

Figure 5.4 Map of the wall at Pungnap-toseong, showing the approximately central location of the Gyeongdang excavation area.

a portion of the urban neighborhood now called Pungnap on the southern bank of the Han River (Figure 5.4). Excavations began in 1997 after the accidental discovery of Baekje artifacts while digging the foundation of a high-rise apartment building, and researchers have continually targeted new demolition/construction projects for the opportunity to study the ancient city (Kwon 2008). Additionally, excavations at the wall itself have sought to more precisely describe the timing and process of its construction, though little dateable material has been forthcoming. Approximately 13 percent of the total site area has been subject to some level of excavation, and efforts are still underway (Kim et al. 2016). Our understanding of Pungnap-toseong and its role in the rising Baekje state is under constant revision as new details come to light.

The fortress walls form an ovoid rectangle with the long walls swelling outward near the center. The approximate north-south axis of the city is tilted to east so as to have the length of its western wall positioned along the river. Although subsequent flooding has destroyed most of the western wall, the other three sides have seen little damage other than minor erosion and cuts made for modern roads. Profiles of the interior of the walls show that they were built in stages, likely beginning in the late third century CE (Kwon 2008). The structure of the city itself is difficult to determine given the available evidence, a total of eighty-six houses found mostly in the east and south, with no palatial or other large structures recovered. An area just north of the city's center, excavated in 2008 and called the Gyeongdang area, contained multiple pits filled in with ceramics and animals remains (Kim et al. 2016). The disposal of cow and horse remains along with dozens of jars, bowls, cooking pots, and other pottery suggest these are disposal areas for feasts, perhaps with their own ritual function in the proceedings.

Compared with contemporaneous sites in the northern Baekje region, houses at Pungnap-toseng contain high levels of both storing and serving vessels, and only moderate amounts of cooking vessels (Kim et al. 2016). Several large storage jars found in both Gyeongdang refuse pits and houses are glazed stoneware of Chinese manufacture (ibid.; SBM-HUM 2011, 2015). The majority, however, are Baekje-produced jars, bowls, lidded vessels, and tripod dishes. Some jars bear the banked linear designs associated with the kiln complex of Sansu-ri, and are likely either imports or imitations of imports. Other decorative techniques from excavated materials include carved and cord-wrapped paddled impressions, impressed triangle and diamond shapes around vessel shoulders, incised wave patterns, and crosshatching (HUM 2006: 250–51). The apparent absence of a ceramic production site in the fortress that has been excavated has led some scholars to hypothesize that all the city's ceramics were provisioned from outside producers (Kim et al. 2016), but given the 87 percent of the site that remains unexcavated, it is safer not to assume this is evidence of absence. Rather, it seems likely that some local production was occurring at, or at least very near, Pungnap-toseong, along with a steady stream of short- and long-distance trading for ceramics and their contents.

All the samples from Pungnap-toseong in this study are from a single feature: Pit 170 in the Gyeongdang area. They represent the ritualized refuse of feasting activities in the central region of the city, and include typical Baekje jars, bowls, and cooking pots, as well as imported Chinese glazewares. Excavated in 2008 along with other, similar features, Pit 170 has not yet been included in the published site reports. Pits 196 and 206, excavated nearby in the same year, can be used as approximations.

The Pungnap-toseong sample is composed of twenty-five gyeongjil sherds, five yeonjil, and twelve of intermediate hardness. Three sherds are glazed, and one other shows the dark exterior surface of a *mayeon* "burnished" blackware. Eleven Pungnap-toseong sherds are decorated with carved-grid tanalmun paddling, and two of these also show marks from a stamp carved with parallel lines. Five more sherds have only the stamped parallel line decoration, though none of these sherds are large enough to exhibit the horizontal rows known from Sansu-ri. Two sherds show cord-wrapped tanalmun paddling, one has linear cord marking that does not appear to be paddle-applied, and one has a small-scale diamond pattern that appears to be applied with a stamp or roulette rather than a paddle. One sherd from the group with parallel line stamps has an air bubble roughly 2 centimeters in diameter from expansion during the firing process. No vessel shapes can be identified from the sherds in the sample.

Jungsan-dong, Yeongjong Island, Incheon Metropolitan City (Gyeonggi Province)

The site of Jungsan-dong lies at the extreme east end of Yeongjong Island, approximately 4 kilometers southeast of Wunbuk-dong. The site was discovered during surveys carried out between 2002 and 2006, and excavation took place from 2007 to 2009, uncovering a Neolithic component of thirty-one dwellings and a single Baekje-era house (HICH 2012a). The Baekje house, though singular, was abandoned due to fire and therefore well-preserved, with artifacts *in situ*. A single AMS taken on wood charcoal from the Baekje house returned a calibrated date of 495 CE (Appendix B), around the end of the Hanseong Baekje period. The house itself is square, roughly 7 meters a side, with postholes in each corner. A hearth is located near the center of the north wall, with the majority of pottery remains nearby in the northeast corner. The ceramic assemblage consists of typical Baekje vessels such as deep bowls, short-necked jars with round bottoms, lug-handled pots, and large storage jars. The largest jar (68 centimeters tall) was found with two iron chisels inside of it, which may have been resting on or near the jar when the fire occurred. Ten more iron tools were found clustered in the center of the house, with more iron tools scattered around the southern side of the house. Slag was recovered from an associated feature with a Baekje date, but no evidence for an iron production location has been found.

The sample from Jungsan-dong presents a fascinating opportunity to examine multiple pots from a single household. A total of twenty-three sherds were collected from the thirty-eight Baekje pots found at the site. Nineteen sherds are from the destroyed house, three from surface collection, and one from a pit feature. These come from a variety of vessel forms, show no consistent firing technique, and are decorated with carved and cord-wrapped paddling, incised parallel lines, and, in two cases, diamond-shaped indentations.

The twenty-three sherds from Incheon Jungsan-dong contain eighteen yeonjil, three intermediate and two gyeongjil. The Jungsan-dong subsample is diverse in decoration, including carved-grid and cord-wrapped tanalmun paddling, dragged comb, incised parallel line, and impressed diamond pattern designs. From contextual information available for roughly half the Jungsan-dong sample, the vessels represented include deep bowls (two), lug-handled pots (two), globular jars (two), a jar, a large jar, and a low jar.

Hanam, Gwangju Metropolitan City (South Jeolla Province)

The Baekje site at Gwangju Hanam was excavated in 2014 and 2015, and like Gwangju Balsan, its excavation report is still being compiled. The site is located in the northwestern portion of the city, away from the densest modern population. Several houses, kilns, and aboveground structures were recovered, along with at least one tomb. The ceramics sampled from Hanam include one sherd from a tomb, one from a ditch outside the settlement, one from a pit feature, and seven from household contexts.

Of the ten sherds from Gwangju Hanam, five are yeonjil, with two gyeongjil and three intermediate. Two yeonjil sherds have carved-grid tanalmun paddling, and two other yeonjil sherds have highly eroded impressions of uncertain origin. Two intermediate sherds are decorated, one with an incised wave pattern in a very small scale, and one with cord markings that are peculiar for showing no knotting of the cord. One gyeongjil sherd has grooves incised parallel to its rim. The pot with the wave pattern is identifiable as a jar, and another sherd is thick and flat, possibly a large jar base or a tile.

GEOLOGY AND GEOCHEMISTRY

Before moving on to the results of the provenience studies on the sites described above, it is important to establish the geological resources available in the vicinity of these settlements. The southwestern Korean Peninsula is composed of a limited number of bedrock formations, making it possible for far-flung clay sources to bear remarkable chemical similarities. The predominant bedrock formation in this region is a late Jurassic granite known as the Daebo formation (Chough 2013; Chough et al. 2000). A second major granite source is the Bulguksa formation from the Cretaceous period. Sedimentary formations and metamorphic gneisses and schists appear with frequency but limited range. The interdigitated nature of these geological sediments means that even nearby sites may have had access to chemically distinct clay sources, even as local pottery from sites hundreds of kilometers distant may be difficult to distinguish.

The area around Gwangju (Figure 5.5) is fairly geologically diverse, but the sites of Balsan, Silye, and Hanam are located on

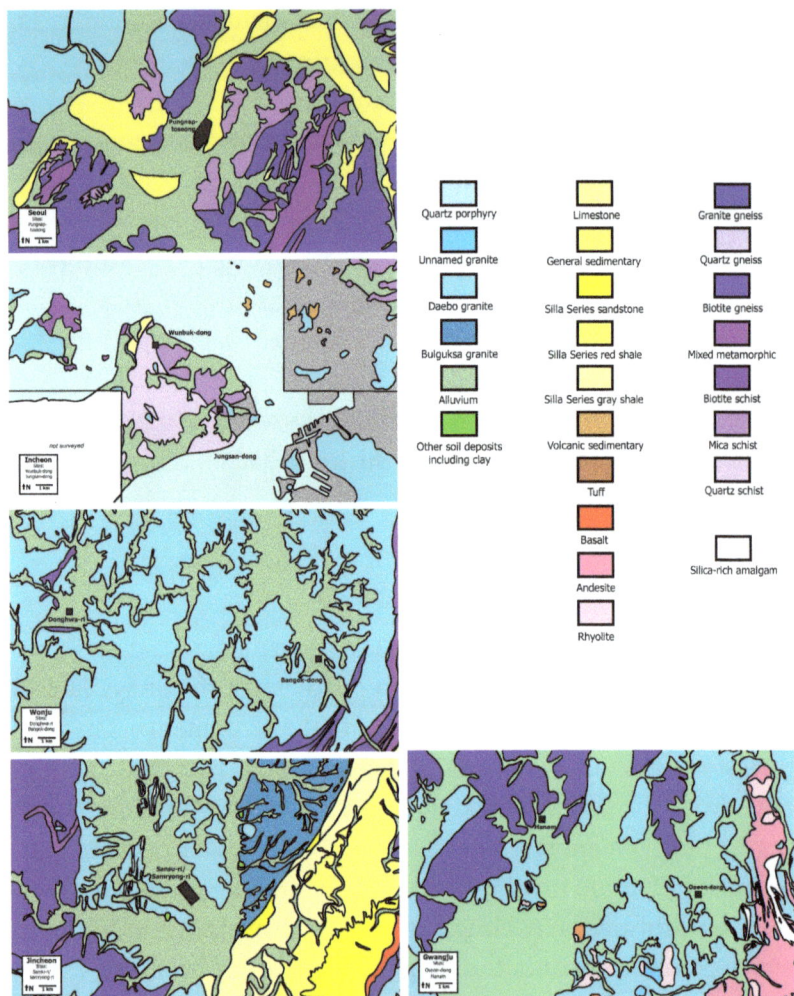

Figure 5.5 Geological maps of the five areas in this study, showing location of sites.

Source: Compiled with data from mgeo.kigam.re.kr (2017).

alluvium near Precambrian granite gneiss, with Daebo granite nearby. To the south of the sites, small pockets of Cretaceous tuff and (non-Bulguksa) granite appear. Deposits of andesite and rhyolite lie to the east of the site, unique among the sites in this study, but at greater than 10 kilometers distant from Balsan, Silye, and Hanam, the contribution of these rocks to the chemistry of clay sources at the sites is questionable.

The two sites in the vicinity of Wonju City have extremely reduced geological resources, as both are situated on alluvial deposits among Daebo granite. Small amounts of biotite schist and gneiss occur near Donghwa-ri, and the gneiss complex of Mt. Chiak abut Bangok-dong to the east. Even with these other formations, the Wonju sites are likely to serve as standards for Daebo granite chemistry.

Small occurrences of Daebo granite dot Yeongjong Island, but do not make up a significant portion of its bedrock. The area surrounding Wunbuk-dong contains quartz and mica schists and a small band of limestone, while Jungsan-dong has slightly more Daebo granite available along with the quartz and mica schists. These formations suggest that clay sources on Incheon may be highly felsic, and the increased silica content would likely read as lower levels of other minerals in INAA data.

The modern towns of Sansu-ri and Samryong-ri are located in alluvial deposits abutting Daebo granite, with a smaller region of Bulguksa granite. Precambrian biotite gneiss and granite gneiss appear to the west and south. To the east of the site lies a band of sedimentary rocks called the Silla Series, more common to North and South Gyeongsang Provinces. This includes red and gray shale as well as red sandstone. Sansu-ri is the only site in this study near a source of Silla Series rocks, though it is not known if the inhabitants utilized clay sources from the weathering shale. If not, the presence of Daebo granite could make Sansu-ri pottery chemically quite similar to the pottery of other regions.

Pungnap-toseong rests on sedimentary rock, with easy access to the Han River's alluvial deposits. The mica schist of the Precambrian Gyeonggi Metamorphic Complex appears to the east of the site, with Gyeonggam gneiss and a minor limestone deposit 4–5 kilometers east. The nearest occurrence of the Daebo granite formation is 3 kilometers northwest, across the Han River. Though the location of pottery production near Pungnap-toseong remains unknown, it is likelier to have been on the same side of the Han River as the city itself. The logistical distance of Pungnap-toseong to the Daebo formation is promising for the establishment of a local chemical signature.

NOTE

1 Several of the larger cities in South Korea are governed separately from their surrounding provinces, and in these cases, the geographically relevant province is listed in parentheses. In this case, Gwangju is not politically associated with South Jeolla Province, but it is entirely surrounded by it.

6

Establishing core groups

The sheer amount of data returned by INAA is both one of its greatest strengths and a major challenge. The number of variables can be overwhelming, and a researcher is called on to examine all elements at once while also extracting geologically relevant information from variations within single variables. In this study, the absence of reference material from previous sampling and analysis presents a blank slate for the detection of groups. This chapter examines the INAA data from a broad perspective, looking for general patterns in the data and building potential groups that will later be tested and considered in archaeological context.

MULTIVARIATE ANALYSIS

The data resulting from INAA on the collected sherds address issues of ceramic production and consumption at multiple scales. Pottery that is similar in chemistry should indicate similarity in geographic origin, even to the point of identifying production at an individual kiln. Since most of the sampled pottery in this study come from habitation and burial sites, however, the groups defined must necessarily be relatively general. These groups are also nested so that a chemical pattern common at a particular site is not only its own group but also a subgroup of a broader regional chemical trend.

With the Korean Peninsula comprising a relatively homogenous geological environment, chemical distinctions among production groups on the peninsula will not be possible to determine simply through bulk mineral content. Peninsular pottery, rather, requires a fully multivariate approach. A straightforward place to start with such a sample is principal components analysis (PCA), which plots all the compositional data in n-dimensional space in order to find the axes of greatest variation (Figure 6.1). For the peninsular pottery in this sample, the first principal component explains 34.4 percent of the variation in the data set, and illustrates some important distinctions. Most of the pottery from sites in Gwangju and Wonju have negative scores in PC1, whereas most pottery from Pungnap-toseong and the kiln complex at Sansu-ri return positive scores. The pottery from Incheon is far more scattered, suggesting that the dimensions that explain variation among the other sites do not function particularly well to explain the variation at Incheon.

While PC1 does manage to separate most of the Mahan site pottery from most of the Baekje site pottery, the larger site from Wonju is culturally Baekje, calling this correlation into question. More likely the cause of this differentiation is the relative presence

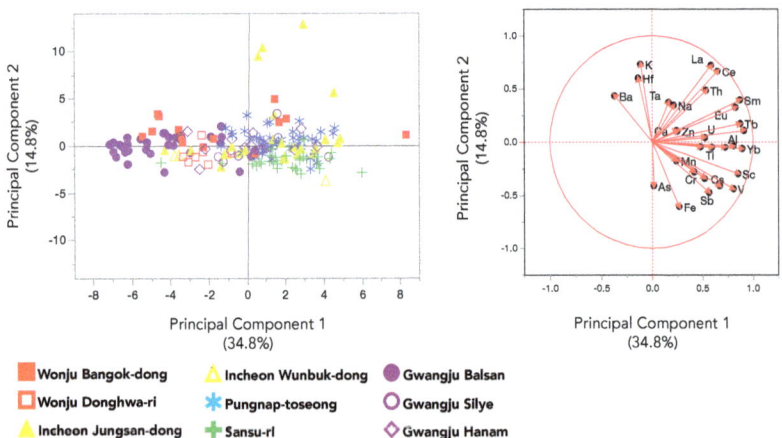

Figure 6.1 Results from Principal Components Analysis (PCA), showing a biplot of PC 1 and PC 2 (left) and the loading plot of all elements (right).

of Daebo granite or, conversely, the relative presence of parent rock other than Daebo granite. This massive granite system underlies the areas around the Wonju and Gwangju sites for kilometers in all directions, with little input from other rock sources. In Seoul and Jincheon, however, a variety of other geological materials suited to clay weathering occur in the vicinity of the sites. A source of shale is present near Sansu-ri, and this is such an ideal clay-forming rock that it may have been part of the reason behind the development of the kiln complex in this location. Other types of sedimentary deposits line the course of the Han River near Pungnap-toseong, weathering and mixing with deposits washing in from upstream.

The first major distinction to be drawn in peninsular pottery is therefore that between Daebo-rich clays (Gwangju and Wonju sites) and Daebo-mixed clays (Pungnap-toseong and Sansu-ri). This does not account for the clays in use at Incheon, and at each of the sites under consideration, more detailed examination of the data will be required to confirm the associations made by PCA. The PCA results, however, do provide a sense of how to move forward in comparisons between sites. As shown in the loading plot in Figure 6.1, most chemicals appear to be more abundant in Daebo-mixed clays. The only elements that occur in higher concentrations in Daebo-rich clays are barium, hafnium, and potassium. The higher levels of potassium, likely from granitic feldspars, are consistent with the hypothesis that Daebo granite has a relatively greater influence on these clays. Hafnium, a heavy metal present in only trace amounts, is more likely variable with location even within the same geological formations. The source of barium is less clear, but does appear to be a signature of much of the pottery at Gwangju Balsan, discussed below.

LOCAL PRODUCTION AT GWANGJU BALSAN AND SANSU-RI

In PCA, the clearest separation in the peninsular sample is between the pots at Gwangju Balsan and those at Sansu-ri. When all samples are subjected to hierarchical cluster analysis (Figure 6.2), Balsan

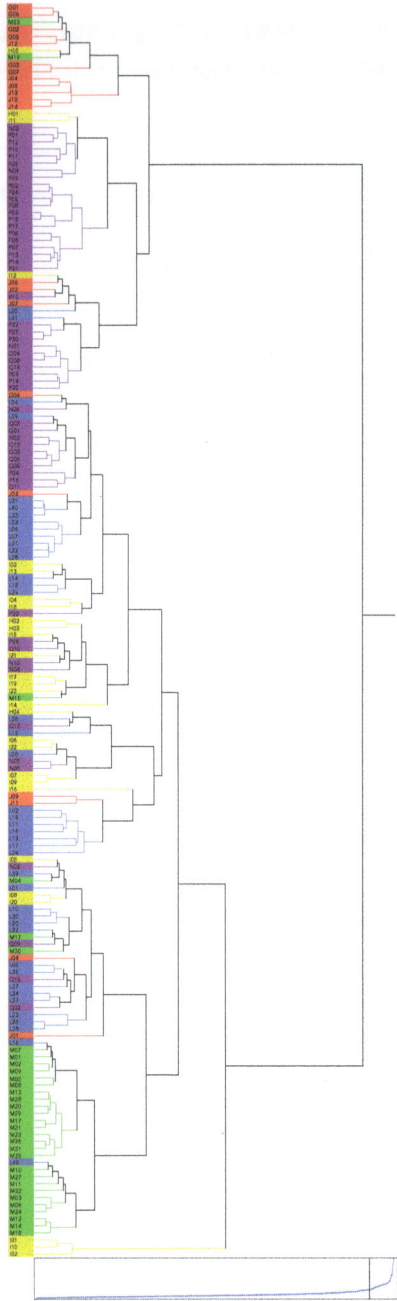

Figure 6.2 Cluster dendrogram generated from 29 elements. Red lines represent sherds from Wonju, green from Sansu-ri, yellow from Incheon, blue from Pungnap-toseong, and purple from Gwangju.

and Sansu-ri also have the distinction of being the least interrupted sets of samples. Twenty-one of Balsan's thirty sherds appear in the same subcluster of Daebo-rich pottery, and twenty-six of Sansu-ri's thirty-two samples comprise a subcluster of Daebo-mixed pottery. The relative internal homogeneity of these sherd assemblages and their chemical distinction from each other make them an ideal starting point for creating geological baselines.

Cluster analysis works by subsequently pairing the most similar observations in a multivariate data set, and is intended to find meaningful groups in the data. This type of analysis is not, however, optimized for geochemical data sets, where none of the variables are truly independent. As seen above, for instance, high concentrations of calcium are correlated with low concentrations of potassium because of the different types of feldspars present in different parent rocks. In addition, elements from the same chemical group tend to covary, particularly the lanthanide sequence, or rare earth elements (REEs). The mathematical abstraction of multivariate analyses can gloss over some of these particularities, but focusing on only a few key elements can fail to provide a full picture of the variation. To round out these two methods, then, the data can be visualized using so-called spider diagrams or "spidergrams" (Rollinson 2014), a technique borrowed from earth sciences in which each sherd is represented by a line moving through the elemental sequence. These spidergrams are particularly useful for visualizing all the trace elements in a sample (excluding neodymium) and allowing direct comparison with the trace elements of other samples. These plots can therefore reveal trends in the data that may stand out to someone with a knowledge of clay chemistry more than they would stand out in a purely mathematical sense.

Viewing the elements side by side in spidergrams, the differences between the Daebo-rich case of Gwangju Balsan and the Daebo-mixed case of Sansu-ri become clear (Figure 6.3). As expected from the PCA loading diagram, the Balsan sherds show peaks in barium and hafnium not seen in the Sansu-ri group, but overall show lower

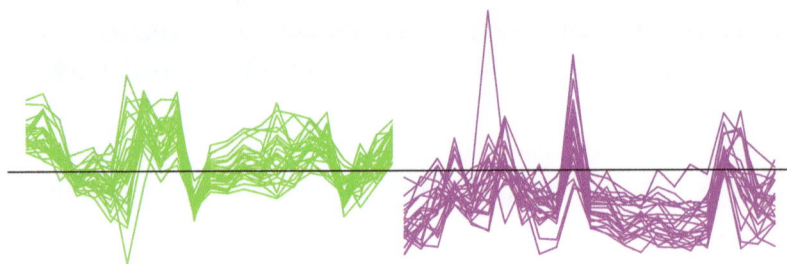

Figure 6.3 Spidergrams comparing trace elements in the local groups from Sansu-ri (left, in green) and Balsan (right, in purple). The Sansu-ri group has higher concentrations of most elements, particularly antimony, rubidium, and cesium, forming the prominent 'M' shape to the left of center. The Balsan group shows consistently higher levels of barium, causing the spike near the center of the graph, and hafnium, causing the spike on the right. Graphs based on standardized data of elements Sc, V, Cr, Mn, Co, Zn, As, Sb, Rb, Cs, Ba, La, Ce, Sm, Eu, Tb, Dy, Yb, Lu, Hf, Ta, Th, and U, with the black line representing 0 on the y-axis.

levels of most elements. Sansu-ri sherds have noticeably high levels of the transition metals scandium and vanadium, as well as major peaks near the center of the plot. Unusually high levels of the metalloid antimony at Sansu-ri could be a peculiarity of the kiln complex's location, and the alkali metals rubidium and cesium likely speak to the clay weathering processes at the site (Kabata-Pendias and Mukherjee 2007: 93–104). Rubidium, the lighter of the two, can replace potassium in silicate minerals like mica, but with stronger bonds. As a rock weathers into clay, then, the potassium disperses at a faster rate than the rubidium. Cesium has similar properties but is even more attracted to the aluminosilicates that make up clays. For both cesium and rubidium, the elevated levels at Sansu-ri are consistent with the hypothesis of a sedimentary parent rock component in the local clay.

The Sansu-ri sherds have consistently elevated REEs relative to Gwangju Balsan, as seen in the sequence from lanthanum to lutetium. The stark drop-off from lutetium to hafnium emphasizes this difference, with Sansu-ri sherds climbing slightly throughout the heavy metal sequence to slightly higher levels of thorium and uranium than at Balsan. Taken together, the relative levels of scandium, vanadium, cesium, rubidium, REEs, and hafnium provide a reliable way to distinguish Sansu-ri pottery from Balsan pottery, and a starting point for comparison with the rest of the peninsular sample. The relationships between pairs of variables that are visualized in spidergrams can be recreated with absolute values by expressing them as ratios; for instance, the ratio of titanium to scandium and the ratio of lutetium to hafnium shown in Figure 6.4 create separation between the core groups that can then be compared to sherds from other sites.

So far, these analytical techniques have repeatedly demonstrated that the sherd assemblages at Sansu-ri and Gwangju Balsan are each relatively internally homogenous, while also being distinct from each other in specific and important ways. The so-called "core groups" of each site are those that exhibit the strongest homogeneity, with several outlier sherds excluded. Some reflection on these core groups themselves is advisable before expanding our view to the other peninsular sites. At Sansu-ri, the homogeneity of geochemistry is easily explained by its known function as a kiln site. Increased specialization often leads to a reduction in variety along both stylistic and compositional variables, and Sansu-ri was certainly a specialized production site. Only four out of thirty-two sherds were not included in this initial definition of the core group, and none of these four stray very far from the typical Sansu-ri chemical pattern. Two have lower overall concentrations of most elements but higher sodium, easily explained by tempering variations, which were confirmed with petrography. One is typical of Sansu-ri in every aspect aside from low levels of cesium and rubidium, and another is only unusual in its low iron content. These variants are of unclear origin but ultimately do not rule out the sherds in question as Sansu-ri products. The unexpected chemical variations in these sherds

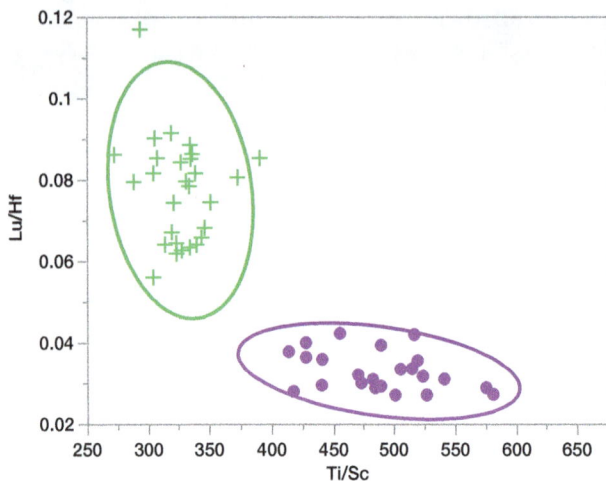

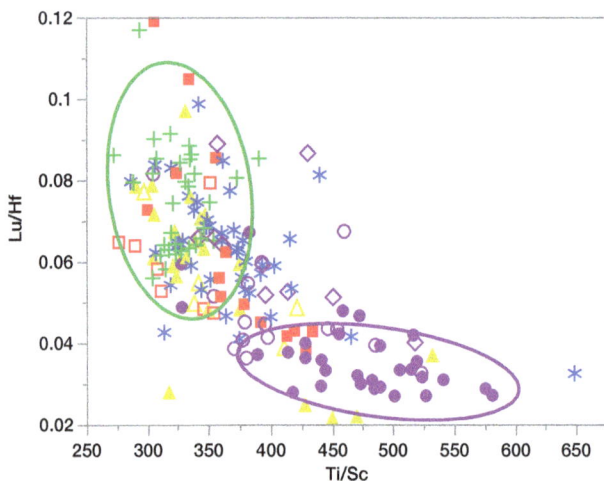

Figure 6.4 Plots of the ratio of titanium to scandium content against the ratio of lutetium to hafnium content. The core groups from Sansu-ri and Balsan are shown with 95% confidence ellipses on their own (top), and with all samples from all sites (bottom).

caused multivariate techniques like PCA and cluster analysis to place them at a distance from their fellows, but the more focused application of spidergrams did not. In fact, when the element ratios identified as particularly salient to this sample are plotted, all four Sansu-ri outlier sherds fall well within the 95 percent density ellipse for the core group (Figure 6.4).

The sherd assemblage from Gwangju Balsan is not uniform to the same degree as Sansu-ri, but Balsan is a residential site with no apparent function for specialized ceramic production. Four sherds out of the thirty can easily be eliminated from the core group, both by multivariate tests and by comparison of spidergrams (Figure 6.5). The overall patterns of variation in these sherds do not match the majority of the Balsan data, and two are noticeably more similar in chemistry to the Sansu-ri sherds. Another three sherds are fairly similar to the remaining twenty-three core group sherds, with the same patterns of bulk minerals, low transition metals, and high hafnium. These three sherds are extremely similar to each other, lower in barium and higher in cesium and rubidium than the core group, and also show extremely low arsenic. This last characteristic is particularly telling, as arsenic sublimates at higher firing temperatures (Cogswell et al. 1996), leaving lower concentrations of arsenic in stoneware vessels. The subgroup of three consists only of gyeongjil-fired sherds, explaining the arsenic variation and hinting at the reason for the deviation in other elements. If the elevated cesium and rubidium result from the mixture of Daebo-derived clays with more plastic clays weathered from shale and other sedimentary rocks, as was the case in Sansu-ri, then these sherds, too, may have been produced at a specialized site located near a quality clay source. Given the similarity in other elements, especially hafnium, this specialized location may not have been far from the Balsan site. This hypothesis does not currently account for the variation in barium, but future clay survey may shed light on this issue. The Balsan core group of twenty-three can therefore be expanded to twenty-six to include this gyeongjil subgroup

Gwangju Balsan

Figure 6.5 Spidergrams comparing the local group at Balsan (light purple in top graph) to the short distance group (top, purple), mid-distance group (middle, green shown with Sansu-ri core group in light green), and long-distance group (bottom, grey). The short distance group is overall more chemically similar, particularly in the heavy elements on the extreme right of the diagram. The mid-distance group is slightly higher in most elements, typical of the northern Mahan/Baekje region. The long-distance group does not follow a similar pattern to any known group. Graphs based on standardized data of elements Sc, V, Cr, Mn, Co, Zn, As, Sb, Rb, Cs, Ba, La, Ce, Sm, Eu, Tb, Dy, Yb, Lu, Hf, Ta, Th, and U, with the black line representing 0 on the y-axis.

when appropriate to both the statistical technique being used and the question being asked.

Several statistical tests exist to determine the appropriateness of multivariate groups once members have been assigned, including techniques such as linear discriminant analysis (LDA) and Mahalanobis Distance. In a large and expanding data set, these tests are useful for identifying outliers and matching new observations to established groups. In a data set of the current size, however, these tests have significant limitations. In order to be mathematically rigorous, each core group should have at least three and preferably five times the number of observations (i.e., sherds) than variables (elements) used in the calculations. With a lower threshold of twenty-three members in the core groups, this would require a reduction of the variables from the full thirty to a mere four or five. One way to deal with this is to use ratios of one element to another, as was done with lutetium and hafnium above, essentially capturing two elements in only one mathematical dimension. When tested using LDA with the variables aluminum, sodium, titanium/scandium, vanadium/chromium, and hafnium/lutetium, no reclassifications were made to the core groups at Balsan and Sansu-ri (Figure 6.6). LDA also provides probabilities for unclassified sherds' membership in the groups, but this test does not allow for the possibility that a sherd belongs to no defined group, so should be treated with caution. Still, LDA

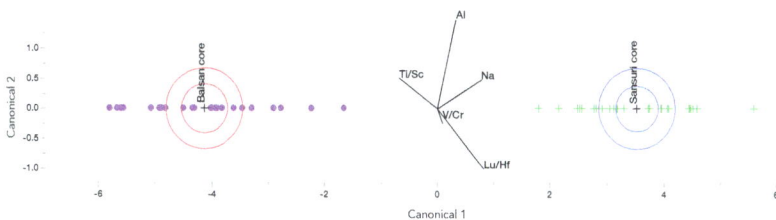

Figure 6.6 Linear discriminant analysis on the core groups from Balsan (purple circles) and Sansu-ri (green crosses). LDA identified no misclassified samples, indicating the groups are mathematically distinct.

provides yet more basis for the next step of analysis: determining which sherds from other sites plausibly belong to the Sansu-ri or Balsan geochemical groups. In the next chapter, I will return the focus to the larger data set, using the established understanding of the core groups at Balsan and Sansu-ri to find additional patterns.

7

THE SOCIAL CONTEXT
OF GEOCHEMICAL VARIATION

The variations in geochemical data have provided a broad understanding of the difference between generally northern and southern geologies in the Mahan/Baekje region, as well as providing intriguing small-scale patterns with important social implications. In this chapter, the process of identifying and testing mathematically sound groups of sherds will articulate with these implications, following some specific assumptions and a context-specific model of scales of distance. The first assumption was implied in the previous chapter: that, all things being equal, the largest chemically similar group of sherds at any given site likely represent local production. This assumption will be overruled in one important case (Pungnap-toseong), but is actively operating at all others. The second is the so-called provenance postulate (Neff 2000; Glascock and Neff 2003), which states that the variation between chemical composition groups should meaningfully exceed the variation within any given group. This is often visualized in data plots by including ellipses representing confidence intervals, demonstrating clearly when groups stand apart from each other. The demands of the provenance postulate have already been met by the core groups at Balsan and Sansu-ri, though Pungnap-toseong will again challenge the application of this principle.

The third assumption in the following analysis is necessary given the limited use of INAA in Korea preceding this study. The true variation in clay chemistry is unknown, and so in many cases I must assume that relative geochemical dissimilarity is equivalent to geographical distance. I have attempted to apply this assumption conservatively, forming a flexible model of distance that can be amended as more data become available. As compositional groups of sherds from individual sites are identified below, they are identified as originating from one of four scales of distance: local, short-, mid-, and long-. These four scales are explicitly cultural and malleable, with the real geographical distance of each changing significantly depending on the site under consideration. (For more detail on the chemical nature and mathematical testing of each composition group, see Walsh 2017.) Local sherds are those that travel little to no distance from producer to consumer, presumably made in kilns at the very site in which they are found. Sherds from the short distance are those produced within the immediate cultural boundary, that is, the Mahan polity to which a site belonged, or for Baekje sites, the entire Baekje kingdom. Mid-distance sherds have a chemistry consistent with the general Mahan/Baekje region, but appear to be from outside the immediate cultural boundary. At a Mahan site, a mid-distance sherd could be from another Mahan polity or from Baekje, and at a Baekje site, a mid-distance sherd is likely from a Mahan culture. Long-distance sherds are those that fall into a known or unknown chemical group outside the local group, including outliers belonging to no group. Outlying samples will be referred to below as "exotic," denoting their origin from outside the focal context, and not intended to connote any strange or beguiling qualities. These sherds may be from the northern or southeastern peninsula, or from societies on mainland or insular East Asia. The distinction between imports from fellow Korean societies and those beyond the peninsula is certainly of great cultural significance, but cannot be determined without greater geological sampling from the broader region.

PATTERNS IN MAHAN CERAMIC DATA

The ceramic sample from the Gwangju Balsan site, though limited to thirty sherds, has significant implications for our understanding of the Mahan political economy. The largest chemical group, identified as local production and its membership confirmed through multivariate tests, can be considered representative of ceramic production that occurred at the settlement itself. The chemistry of this group is reasonably cohesive but with internal variation. Given the relative consistency of the geological environment at Balsan, these slight variations may reflect pots made from various clay sources in close proximity and therefore weathered from the same parent rock, as was the case with the compositional analysis from ethnographically known sources for Kalinga potters by Stark et al. (2000). Local production at Balsan was therefore likely small in scale, with multiple households producing yeonjil wares for use by their own and perhaps nearby kin groups.

The three gyeongjil/intermediate sherds that are now identified as short-distance in origin provide a different perspective on Mahan ceramic production. These three sherds are virtually identical in chemistry and have very uniform pastes, though one (P23) was fired at a somewhat lower temperature than the other two. Both in element profile and in multivariate analysis, the chemistry of these pots appears closely related to the local group at Balsan, but some major differences suggest they were not produced from the same clay source as the local group, but rather a related one. Throughout the Mahan region, kilns are most common at large sites like Balsan and very small sites with only a few houses. A site with as many houses as kilns is a strong indicator of specialization, as this would produce more pottery than the occupants were capable of consuming, and implies a high production output intended for consumption by people external to the settlement. Specialization with a high level of output often results in this sort of observable standardization (Costin 1991), making the hypothesis that the short-distance Balsan sherds came from this type of small kiln complex a reasonable one.

Mahan people therefore had a relatively nonspecialized economy of yeonjil production, and a more specialized system for the production of gyeongjil. Current evidence is insufficient to determine if either of these involved full-time, year-round labor. Yeonjil may have been produced as needed on an intermittent or seasonal basis. Likewise, the specialists producing gyeongjil at small sites may not have occupied the houses there permanently, but moved in and out when weather or social conditions dictated an appropriate time for gyeongjil production. The high degree of standardization in the GJB-near-1 pastes relative to the GJB-local pastes suggests that whoever was making the gyeongjil, they were a defined group of potters who were not considered interchangeable with yeonjil producers.

The social meaning of yeonjil and gyeongjil within a Mahan context is still unclear. Gyeongjil, though produced in a more specialized way, occurs in a seemingly random pattern within Balsan and other Mahan settlement sites, defying any attempt to tie these high-fired wares to social status. Access to gyeongjil does not appear to have been restricted in any way, nor does it appear to have been used by elites to accumulate wealth or prestige. With such a dispersed pattern of consumption, the possibility of elite sponsorship of production is remote, and it seems likeliest that all ceramic craftspeople in this Mahan context were relatively independent, even when specialized. Further investigation into the small kiln sites in Jeolla Province may provide a better understanding of the activities, relationships, and identities of gyeongjil producers.

Four sherds from Gwangju Balsan were not produced either at or nearby the site. Two can be placed with reasonable certainty in the production tradition of the northern Mahan/Baekje region, in or near Gyeonggi Province, and are classified as mid-distance. The final two are from different geological contexts, in regions that remain unknown, and are therefore labeled long-distance. One of these exotic sherds is gyeongjil, one of the mid-distance sherds is intermediate, and the other two are yeonjil. While these sherds indicate the importance of intersocietal trade to Mahan people, it remains unclear whether the pots themselves were considered valuable in this exchange, or if value was assigned to their contents, or if the pots were a less valued consequence of a different, perhaps even ephemeral practice that motivated these exchanges.

The Balsan sherds speak volumes to the living world of ceramic practices, and the sherds from the nearby Silye site have as much to say about pottery that accompanied the deceased. The sherds from Silye did not form as unified group as those from Balsan, but three out of the fifteen were clearly identifiable with the local production group at Balsan (Figure 7.1). An additional two sherds were exotic, and the remaining ten sherds showed some combination of chemical characteristics with typical Balsan and typical Sansu-ri sherds. This suggests that these sherds, along with the two from Balsan that showed Sansu-ri traits, originate from the area between Oseon-dong and Sansu-ri, a distance of 200 kilometers over relatively stable geological terrain. Key to this interpretation is the variation in heavy metal content, particularly lanthanides, which tend to be lower in Gwangju pottery and higher in Sansu-ri, and hafnium, which is higher at Gwangju. Therefore, ten out of fifteen sherds can be identified as originating from the mid-distance, a very different proportion than found at the Balsan settlement.

The majority inclusion of mid-distance pottery in the Silye tombs indicates a set of behaviors reserved for mortuary ritual. While daily life appears to have focused on the local and near-local, these mortuary offerings represent a larger swath of Mahan territory. If we conceive of Mahan as numerous small polities allied through some combination of culture, politics, and economy, then in all likelihood the pots in Silye tombs come mostly from external polities—still Mahan, but not the same Mahan as those living at Oseon-dong. The frequency of mid-distance pottery may indicate the presence of dignitaries and/or kin from these locations at the time of interment. The tombs in question here are monumental, the graves of political leaders or otherwise prominent members of local society. The death of such an individual would certainly have been a major event for the polity, but was apparently also

Gwangju Silye

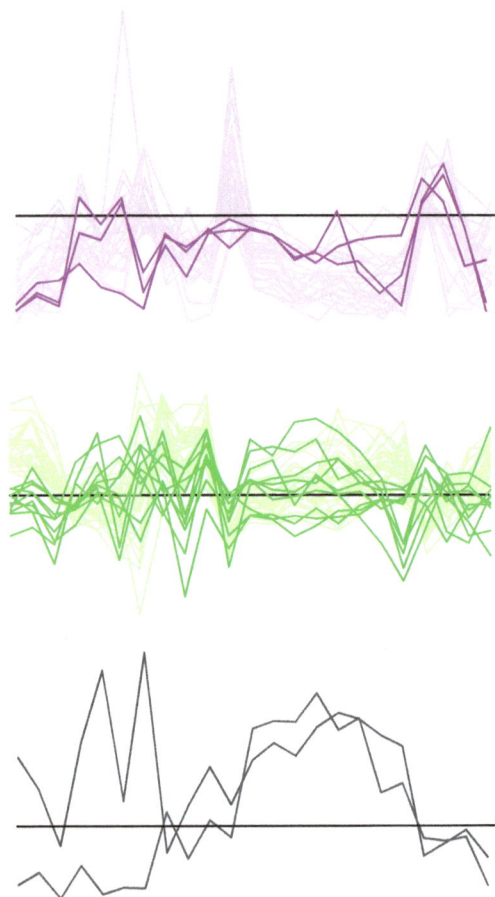

Figure 7.1 Spidergrams of the Silye composition groups. Top, the three sherds belonging to the local group are shown in purple, with the Balsan local group in light purple for comparison. In the center, the ten sherds in the mid-distance group are shown in green, with the Sansu-ri local group shown in light green for comparison. Bottom, the two long-distance sherds in grey show no correspondence to other known groups. Graphs based on standardized data of elements Sc, V, Cr, Mn, Co, Zn, As, Sb, Rb, Cs, Ba, La, Ce, Sm, Eu, Tb, Dy, Yb, Lu, Hf, Ta, Th, and U, with the black line representing 0 on the y-axis.

considered an appropriate time to call on inter-polity relationships and reaffirm the ties that held Mahan groups together. While
no equivalent insight can be gleaned from the Baekje sherd data,
which come entirely from settlements and not tombs, this represents a significant feature of ceramics' role in Mahan social life.

The importance of long-distance exchanges to Mahan society is
perhaps the clearest conclusion that can be drawn from the remaining three Mahan sites in this study (Figure 7.2). Differentiating
local and nearby production at either site in Wonju proved unrelia-
ble due to the variation within the sample and small sample sizes,
but sherds exotic to the general geological environment could still
be identified. At Bangok-dong, the bulk minerals for three sherds
fell outside the parameters for either the Gwangju or the greater
Gyeonggi region, out of fourteen sherds sampled from the site. At
Donghwa-ri, three out of only seven sherds were clearly from a different geological context. Two of these have similar enough chemistry to suppose they originate from the same location, and with their
peaks in cobalt and chromium, that yet unknown source may have
a volcanic component. Five sherds from Incheon Wunbuk-dong
provided a similar challenge in identifying a local signature, but
one sherd matched fairly well with the chemistry of Gwangju Balsan. The artifacts from Wunbuk-dong indicate that the inhabitants
were involved in trade or even culturally associated with the Han
commandery at Lelang. The presence of southern Mahan pottery
in the same site speaks to the extent of the economic relationships.
Whether or not the people at Wunbuk-dong identified as Mahan,
the evidence for long-distance Mahan networks of exchange is
strengthened by this result.

PATTERNS IN BAEKJE CERAMIC DATA

Unlike at the Mahan sites, where standardization and specialization of production could only be inferred from vessel remains, the
Baekje samples provide an excellent economic case study in the
site of Sansu-ri. The numerous kilns and workshops excavated at

Wonju Bangok-dong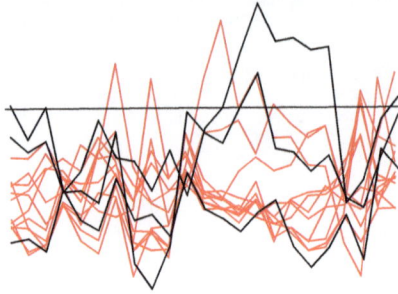

Wonju Donghwa-ri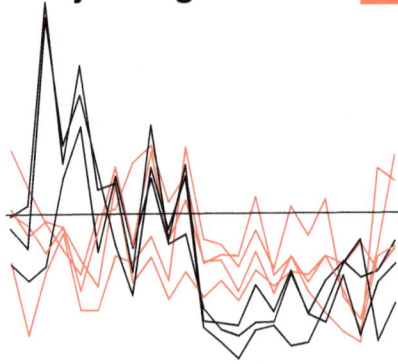

Incheon Wunbuk-dong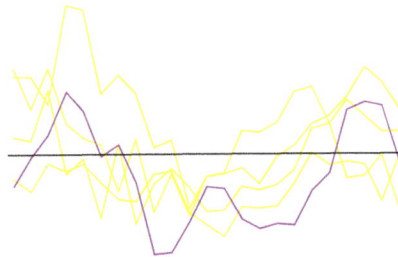

Figure 7.2 Spidergrams of the Mahan sites at Wonju and Incheon. Long-distance imports to the Wonju sites are shown as black lines, and an import resembling the Gwangju local group from Incheon Wunbuk-dong is shown as a purple linc. Graphs based on standardized data of elements Sc, V, Cr, Mn, Co, Zn, As, Sb, Rb, Cs, Ba, La, Ce, Sm, Eu, Tb, Dy, Yb, Lu, Hf, Ta, Th, and U, with the black line representing 0 on the y-axis.

Sansu-ri comprise a nucleated concentration of production at an unprecedentedly high scale for the region. Pots made in the distinctive Sansu-ri style have been recovered from sites throughout the northern Mahan/Baekje region (Seong 2012, 2016), indicating the frequent use of these pots as exchange goods. This may have encouraged production to move to a year-round schedule, if this was not already the case for specialized producers. The composition of production groups is unknown, and the question of whether they remained kin-based must remain open. The techniques for making a Sansu-ri pot appear to be slightly modified from the general Mahan/Baekje tradition, with the inclusion of very small organic inclusions a feature of these pots that does not appear in most southern wares, and is less common in non-Sansu-ri production in the north. The chemistry of sherds sampled from Sansu-ri shows less variation than any other site in the entire sample, with only four out of thirty-two sherds deviating from a clear local signal. Over 70 percent of the sherds are gyeongjil, indicating a high degree of control over firing temperatures for the period. The level of standardization in Sansu-ri is impressive, but the deviations from it provide crucial perspective on the social aspects of production organization.

Of six yeonjil sherds sampled, half of these were excavated from houses rather than kilns. Two gyeongjil and one intermediate sherd were also recovered from houses. Five of the sherds from houses fall squarely into the dominant chemical signature, with important ramifications for the social role of these goods. The specialized potters were producing widely valued goods, and yet they themselves continued to have access to them as consumers. The gyeongjil and intermediate pots from houses, in particular M18, are beautiful specimens of the Sansu-ri style and would presumably have had high value for exchange. Their presence in the houses presumably occupied by these craftspeople indicates not only that these pots were not used exclusively by elite members of Baekje society but also that the potters themselves maintained at least a certain amount of control over the distribution of their goods. While pots produced at Sansu-ri were favored by residents of Pungnap-toseong, their frequent appearance at other sites in Chungcheong and Gyeonggi provinces adds weight to this interpretation. As seen in this study, Sansu-ri pots even appear at the very modest Baekje house in Incheon Jungsan-dong, used as everyday wares. Though seemingly highly sought after by Baekje elites for what appear to be important community rituals, these pots were available to a wide swath of Baekje society, across multiple classes.

One pot from a house context at Sansu-ri did not match the main signal, and deserves close scrutiny. Sherd M19 (Figure 7.3) stands out as different in nearly every form of analysis applied to these pots. In spidergram (Figure 7.4), its chemical composition hovers

Figure 7.3 Photograph of sherd M19 from Sansu-ri, showing exterior decoration in the typical linear style.

Sansu-ri

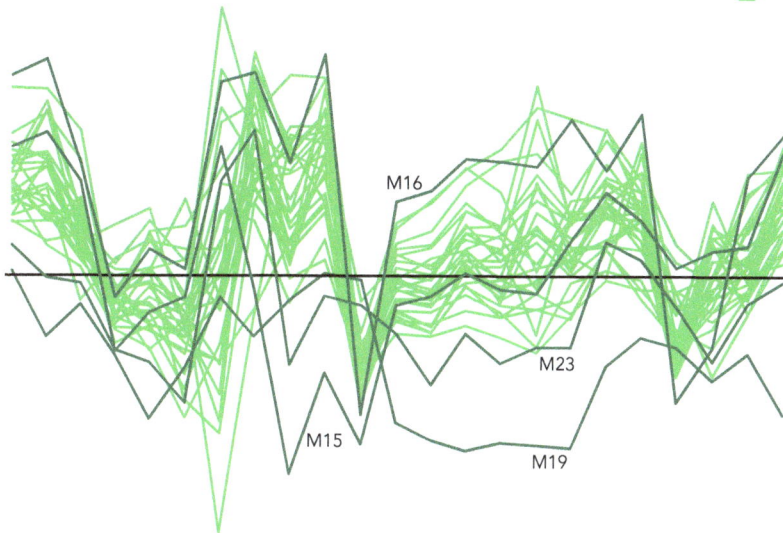

Figure 7.4 Spidergram of all sherds from Sansu-ri, with the main chemical group shown in bright green, and outliers shown in dark green and individually labelled. Graph based on standardized data of elements Sc, V, Cr, Mn, Co, Zn, As, Sb, Rb, Cs, Ba, La, Ce, Sm, Eu, Tb, Dy, Yb, Lu, Hf, Ta, Th, and U, with the black line representing 0 on the y-axis.

below the majority of sherds across most elements; in PCA, the first principal component sends it to the opposite end of the spectrum from its fellows; cluster analysis places it into a different clade at the first level of distinction. LDA could not verify its membership in the Sansu-ri group, yet this sherd bears the stamped parallel lines, arranged in neat rows, that are so distinctive of Sansu-ri style. The difference in chemistry appears to be a straightforward function of paste inclusions. M19 is the only Sansu-ri sherd subjected to petrographic analysis that did not show the small, burnt-out voids indicative of organic temper, and its inorganic inclusions of muscovite mica were very small and very large, with nothing of intermediate size, indicating an intentional addition of material. While this pot was made with a different *chaîne-opératoire* than most Sansu-ri sherds, the sequence was likely modified by an individual potter for a specific purpose. This strange sherd recovered from a craftsperson's house may well have been the result of a desire for a cooking vessel, and the knowledgeable potter opted to add a coarse temper and fire the pot at a low temperature for increased resistance to thermal shock (see Rice 2017: 105). The exclusion of the organic temper may indicate that the use of that material was tied to the desired outcome of a gyeongjil jar, and was considered unnecessary here. This ability for potters to modify the Sansu-ri *chaîne-opératoire* at will and for personal reasons further emphasizes their independence from strict oversight, despite the economic and social importance of their goods. The choice of this potter to adorn the pot with the traditional decoration is a particularly compelling touch, with the potter judging this rather rough-looking vessel worthy of the well-known mark of Sansu-ri technique.

The three other sherds with chemical inconsistencies also likely result from modifications of the Sansu-ri *chaîne-opératoire*, and were all recovered from kiln contexts. M15 is a yeonjil sherd that also has coarser than normal inclusions, and is decorated with paddling rather than stamping, perhaps indicating it too was intended for a use other than as an exchange good. M23 has somewhat coarse inclusions and was only fired to yeonjil hardness (whether intentionally or not), and has beautifully preserved rows of parallel line stamps. M16 is more of a mystery, as its fine-grained paste does not appear different from the main group, but chemically it only shows minor variations. The reduced level of antimony in M16 may simply be the result of variations in the clay source that are not yet understood, rather than any conscious decision making on the part of the potters.

Stylistic consistencies have long persuaded archaeologists that much of the pottery found at the Baekje capital of Pungnap-toseong was transported from Sansu-ri. INAA data bear this out, and the difference in variation in this group compared to the local Sansu-ri group has further implications for the Baekje craft economy. The group of Pungnap-toseong sherds identified as originating from Sansu-ri (Figure 7.5) includes only sherds of gyeongjil and intermediate hardness, with no yeonjil sherds. This aligns with the evidence that Sansu-ri's yeonjil wares were not produced with

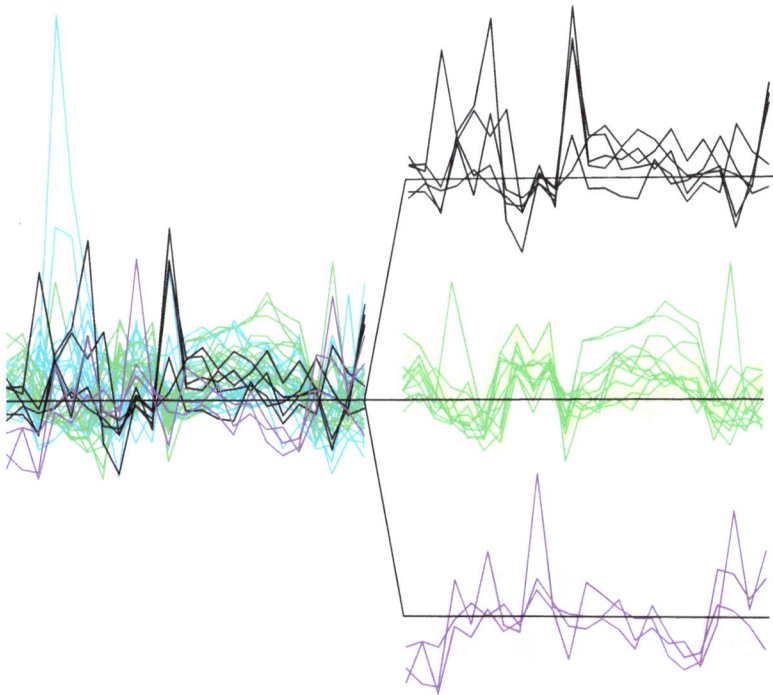

Pungnap-toseong

Figure 7.5 Spidergram of Pungnap-toseong's chemical groups, with all samples shown together on the left, and short-, mid-, and long-distance groups on the right. Long-distance imports with no known origin are shown in black, samples that likely originate from Sansu-ri are shown in green with the Sansu-ri core group in light green for comparison, and samples that likely originate from the Gwangju area are shown in purple with the Balsan core group in light purple for comparison. Graphs based on standardized data of elements Sc, V, Cr, Mn, Co, Zn, As, Sb, Rb, Cs, Ba, La, Ce, Sm, Eu, Tb, Dy, Yb, Lu, Hf, Ta, Th, and U, with the black line representing 0 on the y-axis.

the intention of use in exchange, and that gyeongjil and gyeongjil-like vessels were considered more valuable. The nature of this value is further complicated by the Pungnap-toseong assemblage, as some of the Sansu-ri vessels are not of especially high quality. Two have obvious flaws: sherd L27 has a large mineral inclusion breaking through to the exterior surface, with a pattern of cracks surrounding it roughly 1 centimeter across; sherd L39 has a large air bubble in the vessel wall, roughly 3 centimeters in diameter. However the value of these goods was negotiated, it was not so tied to their quality that flaws such as these were seen as antithetical to their use by the Baekje elites, in a context roughly 80 kilometers from their production origin.

A further clue to the issue of value may lie in some of the more surprising results from INAA. Three sherds in the Pungnap-toseong assemblage had glazed surfaces (Figure 7.6), two with a smooth but mottled glaze (L31 and L33), and one with three distinct drips (L30). While prior to analysis these were assumed to be exotics, their element profiles suggested a much closer origin. The two with mottled glaze were placed in the Sansu-ri group, and this was

Figure 7.6 Sherds L30 (left) and L33 (right) from Pungnap-toseong, showing rudimentary glazes in the form of drips (left) and a mottled surface (right).

confirmed with LDA. L30, the sherd with glaze drips, looked gene-
rically Gyeonggi-like in spidergram, and while multivariate analysis
could not place it definitively into a composition group, a domestic
origin seems likely. No glaze wares have been recovered from the
kilns at Sansu-ri (HUCM 2006), though it would be expected that
experimentation with such technologies would result in mistakes,
identifiable archaeologically as wasters. Possibly this highly specialized production occurred in a very small area in the Sansu-ri complex, and this area has not been sampled. Given the distribution of
flawed vessels discussed above, it is also possible that no mistake
was disastrous enough to render a glazed vessel valueless as an
exchange good, however unlikely that may seem. Caution will be
taken with any attempt at explanation for this phenomenon until
a better understanding of the Gyeonggi region geological variation
can be reached.

Three sherds from Pungnap-toseong bear at least some resemblance to the Balsan group, and may originate from the mid-distance
in Jeolla or Chungcheong. These were tested for membership in the
Balsan composition group, and two gyeongjil sherds met the necessary criteria. The sherd that did not, L09, is a red yeonjil sherd, and
this may have affected the results. Membership in the Balsan composition group does not itself imply that a sherd was produced at
Gwangju Balsan or even very nearby, as the variation in soil chemistry for the Jeolla region was not thoroughly tested and remains unknown. If clays across the Jeolla region are as homogenous as those
in greater Gyeonggi area, then these sherds may have originated in
any place on that landscape. The gyeongjil groups from Gwangju
Balsan were all highly covariant, and the three Pungnap-toseong
sherds are similar but not identical in spidergram. Gyeongjil production methods were more standardized at Gwangju Balsan than
yeonjil, and this standardization may have been more consistent
across a wider area than would have been the case for yeonjil. This
would result in gyeongjil sherds from Jeolla (or whatever region of
Jeolla shares a similar chemistry with Gwangju Balsan) showing
greater chemical similarity than the yeonjil sherds across the same

region. Multivariate methods would be particularly sensitive to this, as seen at Sansu-ri, where the addition of heavy temper in one sherd (M19) excluded it from the main group despite general chemical similarities. This could help explain why a yeonjil sherd that originated from Jeolla but not specifically from Gwangju Balsan would be excluded in LDA, even though this sherd shares several key traits with other southern sherds. This ambiguous result is in fact encouraging for future research, as it implies that difference yeonjil sources in Jeolla may be distinguishable though INAA with sufficient sample size.

An additional five sherds from Pungnap-toseong can be identified as the result of long-distance exchange. Two have bulk minerals outside the norm for the peninsula, and the other three do not resemble the other sampled sherds in the heavier elements. While the identification of exotics from unknown sources involves a certain margin of error, the proportion of sherds from long-distance sources in Pungnap-toseong does not appear to be much higher than that in Gwangju Balsan (Figure 7.7). Rather, the sharpest differences between these two large settlements are seen in the nearer distances, and the consumption of gyeongjil versus yeonjil.

At Pungnap-toseong, the most easily identified groups are those originating from elsewhere, whether that be Sansu-ri, the Jeolla

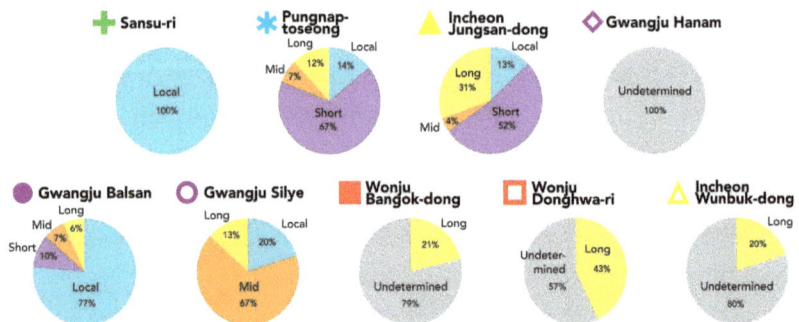

Figure 7.7 Pie charts showing the proportion of sherds from various distances at each site. While local groups could not be identified at all sites, long-distance imports are evidenced at each Mahan site.

region, or further afield. The difficulty appears when attempting to identify local and near-local production. The groups identified as such here do not quite meet the requirements of the "provenance postulate" laid out by Neff (2000). The greater Gyeonggi region's geology may not be varied enough to provide easily identifiable clay source signatures, at least not at this sample size. A small group identified as local and two groups of only two or three sherds that may represent short-distance exchange appear relatively consistent in this noisy Gyeonggi context, but are ultimately too small to be tested statistically. Further INAA testing in this region may elucidate these patterns, but for now I infer that much of the pottery at Pungnap-toseong that did not come from Sansu-ri likely came from other sites in the surrounding region. The pottery moving into Pungnap-toseong from these geologically similar sources included yeonjil, gyeongjil, and intermediate wares, and the precise geographic origins of these wares are still unclear. Some may be locally produced, but without evidence of kilns at Pungnap-toseong, even that much is conjectural.

Evidence for long-distance exchange is plentiful at Incheon Jungsan-dong, in the single Baekje house that contributed twenty-three sherds to analysis (Figure 7.8). One sherd shows a likely origin in Jeolla province (I11), and seven sherds were identified as long-distance due to their variant geochemistry. The bulk minerals of these sherds are not out of the ordinary for the peninsula, but they are strikingly different in other ways. Sherd I16, for instance, was given its own clade in cluster analysis because of thorium and uranium levels roughly 2.5 times higher than average. Interestingly, none of the long-distance sherds appear to have the same origin, but all of the short-distance sherds occur in groups of at least two. This seems to suggest the maintenance of relatively stable exchange relationships with closer communities, and a more opportunistic approach to long-distance trade. The house at Jungsan-dong itself is modest, and the vessels all appear to have been in use as everyday culinary and/or storage wares, including two Sansu-ri gyeongjil vessels. Once again, this provides evidence

Incheon Jungsan-dong

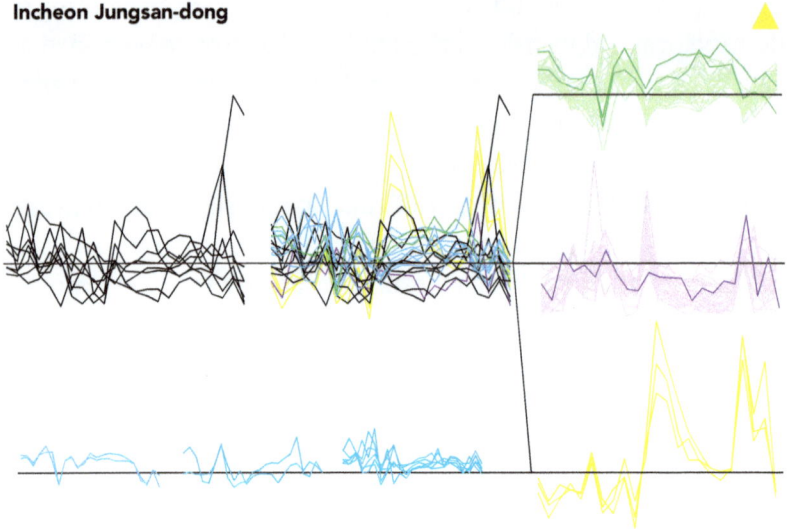

Figure 7.8 Spidergrams of the chemical groups at Incheon Junsan-dong, with all samples shown in the top center graph, long-distance imports of unknown origin on the top left in black, samples that likely originate from Sansu-ri on the top right in green with the Sansu-ri core group in light green for comparison, and samples that likely originate from the Gwang-ju area on right center in purple with the Balsan core group in light purple for comparison. Three samples that were likely made locally are shown bottom right in yellow, and three groups of samples that likely originate from the Gyeonggi region are shown in blue on the bottom left. Graphs based on standardized data of elements Sc, V, Cr, Mn, Co, Zn, As, Sb, Rb, Cs, Ba, La, Ce, Sm, Eu, Tb, Dy, Yb, Lu, Hf, Ta, Th, and U, with the black line representing 0 on the y-axis.

that exchange relationships were culturally valuable to Mahan and Baekje people, but that the pottery involved in these exchanges may not have carried a great deal of that value.

The results from Gwangju Hanam are, unfortunately, little help in understanding the patterns seen in Mahan and Baekje ceramic production, distribution, and consumption. Hanam is a Baekje site established in a culturally Mahan area, but its pottery does not have a clear affiliation with either the nearby site of Gwangju Balsan or

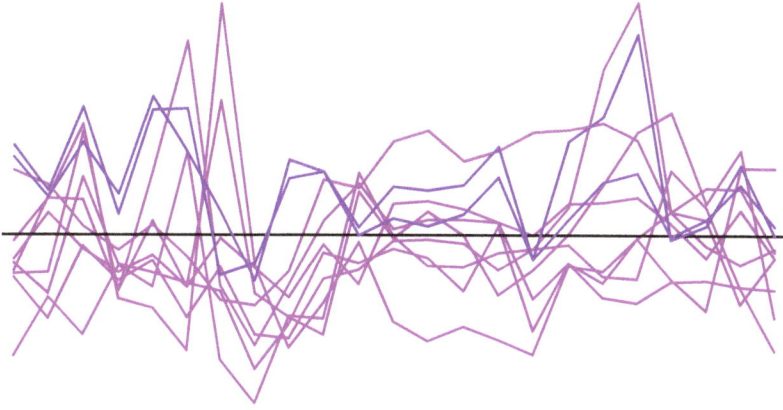

Figure 7.9 Spidergram of all samples from Gwangju Hanam, with two chemically similar sherds shown in darker purple. Graphs based on standardized data of elements Sc, V, Cr, Mn, Co, Zn, As, Sb, Rb, Cs, Ba, La, Ce, Sm, Eu, Tb, Dy, Yb, Lu, Hf, Ta, Th, and U, with the black line representing 0 on the y-axis.

the greater Gyeonggi region (Figure 7.9). Only two of the sherds, No7 and No8, have any strong resemblance to each other. The variation internal to the Hanam sample and its failure to group with any known sources are problems without clear answers. Until more sherd samples can be obtained and a more high-resolution understanding of the geological environment be reached, the Hanam site cannot contribute to broader conclusions about Mahan and Baekje societies.

8

DISCUSSION

SPECIALIZATION, VALUE, AND EXCHANGE

One question has been raised several times in the above discussion: What was the value of these craft goods in the societies that produced, exchanged, and used them? This problem can only be satisfactorily addressed with a more focused look at how value is created within social contexts. Appadurai's (1986) groundbreaking work on the subject argued that the value of an object is ultimately the sum of what an individual is willing to sacrifice for it, and this value is created socially, not economically. The sets of knowledge used to produce an object and to consume that object can become more distinct as the locations of production and consumption become geographically separated, leading Appadurai (2005) to further argue that production and consumption must be considered together. Appadurai's definition of a commodity as a good produced for the intention of exchange is less helpful in this discussion, as the presumption of this intent is too reductive for the complicated scenario observed in the data.

Although it is frequently cited in the archaeological literature, the distinction between utilitarian/subsistence goods and wealth/ prestige goods is somewhat fuzzy in the Mahan/Baekje data. Brumfiel and Earle (1987: 4) drew a boundary between goods used to meet basic household needs and those used in "display, ritual, and exchange," a useful concept but one that may oversimplify the role of ceramics in people's lives. While the terminology has been flexible, this dichotomy is popular in archaeology as a way to examine the changes in craft production and consumption when elite classes are present in a society (Costin 2001; Hayden 1998; Helms 1993; Junker 1999; Peregrine 1991). As Flad and Hruby (2007) pointed out, however, the labels of prestige and utilitarian are not mutually exclusive when applied to objects. Making a thing into a symbol of power or prestige requires its use as such, and is contingent on behaviors involving the object that are recognized as meaningful in social context. A craft good can therefore be highly prestigious at one moment and wholly utilitarian the next, and the attempt by archaeologists to identify one class of ceramic vessels as either prestigious or not is often misguided. Costin (2007) went so far as to say that the concept of value should be replaced with that of function, focusing on observable patterns of consumption and not artifact traits that may signify more to the archaeologist than to the community that produced and used these objects.

The value of pottery depending on specific patterns of use can help explain why Sansu-ri gyeongjil jars appear in nonelite contexts, as the elite behaviors and not the pots themselves were what was inaccessible to these craftspeople. This does not, however, explain why elites at Pungnap-toseong went to the trouble of importing so many pots from Sansu-ri. Economic exchange can be manipulated by elites for a variety of purposes (Brumfiel and Earle 1987; Hirth 1996; Smith 2004; Vaughn 2006), but these have generally required class-based restrictions on consumption that are not supported by the Mahan/Baekje data. Helms (1993) emphasizes long-distance exchange as a venue for elites to reinforce their connection to places both literally and figuratively "beyond," but this need not be restricted to elites. Pailes (2016) demonstrates that emergent elites need not monopolize long-distance exchange networks, and that complexity can involve small-scale exchanges of relatively mundane goods in order to maintain social alliances. In this vein, I argue that the Mahan and Baekje ceramics demonstrated by compositional analysis as exchange goods were ascribed value largely by the distance of their origin. Multiple scales of physical distance were involved in these exchanges, and the value of these distances is also multiscalar and dynamic. While long-distance exchange is evidenced from the majority of sites in this study, the value of distance also played out on the intrasocietal level, with the production of gyeongjil occurring away from major population centers in both Mahan and Baekje for the purpose of social alliances and territorial integration. At the same time, the choice of gyeongjil rather than yeonjil to be produced at this distance was closely related to a cultural sense of appropriateness for special things to come from outside the immediate community. This pattern is visible in Mahan settlements, where evidence for strict social classes and centralized leadership is lacking, and carries over into the Baekje period, where the same cultural underpinnings of prestige in distance were used by elites to consolidate political control.

These findings have many potential ramifications, including insight into the mechanisms of alliance among Mahan cultures, and the ways these groups resisted state formation during the Hanseong Baekje period. Mahan peoples' expertise in long-distance trade has long been acknowledged, and was likely a critical part of Mahan identity construction. Within Mahan territory, however, the movement of goods appears to have occurred under specific, culturally approved circumstances. Vessels used in daily life came from near, far, and places in between, but the focus was on the immediate community and its nearby hinterland. Mortuary activities, on the other hand, drew on a broader sense of identity, and reinforced bonds among neighboring Mahan groups. This continued well after the creation of the Baekje state from Mahan polities in the Han River region to the north, indicating a clear and conscious choice by southern Mahan cultures to remain loosely allied rather than to centralize. Mid- and long-distance ties played into both daily life and mortuary ritual, but on the whole, Mahan polities preferred to retain their individual identities and prioritize their own communities.

MAHAN POLITICAL ECONOMY

All Mahan sites have strong evidence for long-distance trade involving ceramics, regardless of the size or the site or the presence of gyeongjil vessels. This imported pottery was the result of trade networks cultivated among individuals and perhaps sustained over long periods, as suggested by the two sherds from Wonju Dongwha-ri with the same exotic origin. Long-distance trade may have been an essential component of Mahan identity. In the fifth and sixth centuries, keyhole-shaped tombs resembling those famously built in Kofun Japan appear in Jeolla province, a development that Lee (2014) sees as a Mahan invocation of close ties with Japanese societies. The use of these tombs was a localization of the exotic intended in part to intimidate societies like Baekje, to remind nearer neighbors of their importance in the peninsula's connection with the Archipelago. The presence of traded wares at small Baekje sites indicates that the prestige available through such exchange was maintained by numerous individuals at various locations in the Mahan landscape, and was never exclusive to elites.

The larger Mahan site at Gwangju Balsan does not have a higher proportion of long-distance pottery than the smaller sites, but it does have gyeongjil. Large Mahan sites show weak internal differentiation, if any, in terms of house size and the designation of higher- and lower-status precincts. The exclusivity of Mahan gyeongjil to this large site, however, suggests that the ware was considered more appropriate to a town setting and its inhabitants. Its consumption does not appear to have been restricted to any particular group of individuals beyond that, and the production of it at a distance, as seen at Gwangju Balsan, may have been tied to the social justification for its production. Just as exchange relationships with distant communities reinforced social ties in a way that could be wielded as cultural capital, this decentralized production strategy would have served to maintain domestic cohesion economically, politically, and socially. This fits with the historical picture of a Mahan polity as a political unit with a distinct identity, where villages and towns with a dispersed power structure maintained unity through various rituals and events (Yi 2009). Some level of town sponsorship may have been involved in gyeongjil production to ensure that specialists had the means to make these wares and bring them into town, but the pots themselves were not as important as the practice of this exchange. At some point in the use life of a short-distant imported gyeongjil vessel in Gwangju Balsan, it may have been a highly prestigious good, but this status was likely temporary. After this prestige function had been served, the consumption of such a vessel was available to any Mahan town resident.

BAEKJE POLITICAL ECONOMY

If the prestige of ceramics in Mahan society was largely symbolic of social and political relationships, this was modified in Baekje to include a greater degree of economic control. The specialized producers at Sansu-ri were able to make pots for their own use and maintain some or all control over distribution, but the sherds from Sansu-ri do not show any signs of long-distance imports. This likely indicates Sansu-ri's integration into the Baekje economy, and a break with Mahan tradition of long-distance exchange as a common practice across social classes. Whether these individuals now found sufficient prestige in their role as specialized craftspeople or whether long-distance trade was restricted in their new political environment is unclear.

Sansu-ri is far enough from Baekje's cultural core on the Han River that it may have been the southern boundary of territorial control in the early Hanseong period (ca. 300–475 CE). Baekje elites' choice to transport so much of this pottery to Pungnap-toseong may have had as much to do with that distance as with the quality of the vessels, as it displayed and reinforced their authority over an unprecedentedly large region. The jars brought in from Sansu-ri did not need to be flawless to fill this role, explaining why there was no distaste for an air bubble or small crack here and there. Meanwhile, pottery from other nearby areas was also transported to Pungnap-toseong, again as both a Mahan-style strategy for maintaining internal social relationships and a Baekje strategy for integrating the economy. Maintaining and amplifying the decentralized pattern of gyeongjil production may have been a crucial component of political centralization for early Baekje leaders. Further analysis of Baekje sites around Pungnap-toseong will reveal whether this economic integration also came with changes in patterns of long-distance trade, due to social restriction or dwindling interest.

The changing intentions of importing domestic pottery at Pungnap-toseong are also apparent from the context from which these vessels were recovered. Kim et al. (2016) have demonstrated that households at Pungnap-toseong consumed more pottery than those at other Baekje sites in Gyeonggi, particularly serving and storage vessels. The samples in this study come from the remains of ritualized feasting, suggesting that the pots were on full display to a gathered group of people and then purposefully destroyed. Alongside the vessels from politically Baekje sites, pots from Mahan territories and unknown long-distance origins were interred in this pit near the center of the site. Baekje's multiple scales of prestige and control were present in the form of these pots, which were then removed from the possibility of further use. In this case, the symbolism of the objects was far from ephemeral, and Baekje elites sent the message that they had particular access to and control over these connections.

Despite this, the house at Incheon Jungsan-dong maintained its own short-, mid-, and long-distance connections, evidenced by a pattern of ceramic consumption that is strikingly Mahan, give or take a Sansu-ri jar. The location of this site on an island at the important port of Incheon raises the possibility that these goods were accumulated through household members' involvement in sea and land trade, whether incidentally or as a primary means of subsistence. In this way, they may have had access to these wares similar to how Sansu-ri producers kept some of their own pots, with proximity increasing the mundanity of objects that were valuable in other contexts. The staggering amounts of exchanged goods, however, thoroughly undercut any idea of a Baekje elite monopoly on the social and economic connection implied by these wares. While Baekje elites' use of pottery took new forms with new meanings, the established practices of accumulating ceramic goods from multiple distant origins persisted, at least in this coastal settlement.

MAHAN AND BAEKJE AS COMPLEX SOCIETIES

Focusing on leadership strategies and increasing centralization would miss a great deal of the social organization present in both Mahan and Baekje societies. Social differentiation in the Mahan is subtle both vertically and horizontally, with the distribution of ceramics in sites pointing to both equalities and inequalities. The consumption of gyeongjil was more available to people living in large towns than those in villages, and as gyeongjil was produced at a distance from these towns, this may indicate the perceived importance of towns in the management of the Mahan polity as a whole. Long-distance trade, an important component of Mahan culture, was practiced by individuals in small settlements as well as large ones, and does not appear to have been the subject of social proscription, elite or otherwise.

Baekje, a historically known kingdom, is often studied in terms of its relationship to China and Chinese statecraft. The ceramic data presented here cannot speak to that relationship, as even some glazed sherds that were presumed Chinese in origin appear to have been produced domestically. Rather, these data show that Baekje elites elaborated Mahan practices in importing gyeongjil wares from the far reaches of their control for use in larger settlements, in this case the walled site of Pungnap-toseong. The use of vessels imported from various distances served an important function in Baekje rituals, and was accompanied by a level of economic integration well beyond the Mahan precedent. Consumption patterns from outside Pungnap-toseong, however, demonstrate that the use of this valued pottery was not exclusive to Baekje elites or city dwellers. Trade with communities both domestic and foreign also remained open to nonelites, at least in some cases, and was not exclusively controlled by the centralized Baekje political structure during the Hanseong period. A purely hierarchical approach to Baekje statecraft would gloss over these intricacies, and minimize the extent to which the Baekje economy proceeded from a Mahan model. Looking at Baekje as a complex society with the expectation of both hierarchical and heterarchical organization reveals a political economy with multiple nodes of power and control, resulting from local people making decisions in a locally situated cultural context.

CONCLUSION

This study represents the first time ceramic materials from a southern Mahan settlement have been subjected to INAA, and the inclusion of samples from sites of multiple sizes and functions in Mahan and Baekje has allowed interpretations of the hierarchical and heterarchical complexity of these societies. By establishing chemical signatures unique to specific production locales within the region, this study invites further research to build on these conclusions, and further interrogate the role of ceramics in the function of Mahan and Baekje societies. Moving forward, traditional views on Baekje will need to be reconsidered, as the kingdom clearly deployed autochthonous political, economic, and social strategies to integrate and administer its territory, rather than relying on imported Chinese bureaucratic models. All the more will Mahan's role in Korean prehistory and history require revision, an effort begun by numerous scholars working on the southern Mahan region (Kim S.-O. 2014; Lee 2014; Lee Y. C. 2011; Yim 2014).

The Mahan polities of North and South Jeolla provinces have become the focus of this conceptual shift simply for their existence after the establishment of the Baekje kingdom, and for the various ways in which they maintained local authority and identity at a time of great social change. Mahan culture is an excellent example of social complexity in a nonevolutionary sense, as it both did and did not develop into a state-level society. The northern Mahan polities, for whom the warring groups in the northern Peninsula posed a far more immediate threat, unified into the Baekje kingdom in a process not directly addressed by the data in this study. Baekje's statecraft, however, can be seen in the patterns of ceramic production, exchange, and consumption described here, and was based on Mahan models of political economy. The southern Mahan groups did not remain unchanged at this time, but persisted as Mahan in material culture and political organization, with some alterations that may have been intended to further distance themselves from Baekje by reinforcing their own local authority.

While this understanding of Mahan's sustained autonomy has only gained ground in the past few years, Mahan cultures were not the only Three Kingdoms societies in Korea that did not follow a trajectory toward statehood. The nearby Gaya polities have been somewhat more thoroughly studied as an example of a group of allied polities that resisted the trend toward political centralization in the fourth and fifth centuries CE (Byington 2012). According to historical narratives, Gaya was ultimately conquered by the expansive Silla kingdom, and remained decentralized even when that may have been a disadvantage against Silla forces. The development of a nonstate complex society into a state is not only not inevitable, it is often not desired, and resisted both culturally and militarily. Although not as frequently mentioned in historical documents, Mahan has shown itself to be a further Korean example of stalwartly constructed and maintained nonstate identity in a region and time when multiple states were eager to expand their territory and influence.

Questions on the organization of the Baekje state have most often been approached from a historical perspective, with texts surviving from Japanese and Chinese societies as well as the Korean kingdoms that ruled southwestern Korea after Baekje's demise. These histories prioritize elite activities and relationships, and portray an administrative bureaucracy from the later Baekje periods that is in turn taken as typical of Baekje's entire existence (Best 2006). Archaeological evidence can supply information on the lives of people outside the elite classes, and is particularly necessary in Baekje, where locally produced textual records have been lost. The results presented here ultimately underline the Mahanness of the early Baekje state, with power dispersed across multiple social classes, and an economy based in heterarchical structures as much or more than hierarchical ones. As research in this vein continues, broader issues in the relationship between Mahan and Baekje can be addressed, such as the means by which emerging Baekje elites constructed a cultural identity separate from the Mahan while expanding into Mahan territories and maintaining social, political, and economic ties with the remaining Mahan polities. Baekje's defeat at the end of the Hanseong period and retreat south only further complicated its relationship with Mahan, ushering in a time when social status and identity must have been highly dynamic. Excavations in Chungcheong and Jeolla provinces will continue to provide evidence of these processes, and with sufficient data, scholars will be able to determine why, how, and if Baekje culture managed to replace Mahan in these reaches in the sixth and seventh centuries CE.

The possibilities for future research in Korea using INAA are manifold, including expanding the samples both geographically, to observe contemporaneous trends in other Korean societies, and temporally, to provide information on how ceramic production traditions changed through time. This research would also be enhanced by clay survey in the regions under study, to detect patterns of resource use and provide better data on how raw materials were treated and mixed by ancient potters. Ultimately, collaboration with colleagues in Korea, Japan, China, and beyond will assist in building a more complete picture of craft production and interregional interactions in ancient East Asia.

References Cited

Alden, John R., and Leah Minc. 2016. "Itinerant Potters and the Transmission of Ceramic Technologies and Styles during the Proto-Elamite Period in Iran." *Journal of Archaeological Science: Reports* 7: 863–76.

Appadurai, Arjun. 1986. *The Social Life of Things: Commodities in Cultural Perspective*. Cambridge: Cambridge University Press.

———. 2005. "Materiality in the Future of Anthropology." In *Commodification: Things, Agency, and Identities*, edited by Wim M. J. van Binsbergen and Peter Geschiere, 55–62. Münster: Lit Verlag.

Arnold, D. E. 2000. "Does the Standardization of Ceramic Pastes Really Mean Specialization?" *Journal of Archaeological Method and Theory* 7 (4): 333–75.

Arnold, Dean E., Hector Neff, and Ronald L. Bishop. 1991. "Compositional Analysis and Sources of Pottery: An Ethnoarcheological Approach." *American Anthropologist* 93 (1): 70–90.

Arnold, Dean E., Hector Neff, Ronald L. Bishop, and Michael D. Glascock. 1999. "Testing Interpretive Assumptions of Neutron Activation Analysis." In *Material Meanings: Critical Approaches to the Interpretation of Material Culture*, edited by Elizabeth S. Chilton, 61–84. Salt Lake City: University of Utah Press.

Baines, John, and Norman Yoffee. 1998. "Order, Legitimacy, and Wealth in Ancient Egypt and Mesopotamia." In *Archaic States*, edited by Gary M. Feinman and Joyce Marcus, 199–260. Santa Fe, NM: School of American Research Press.

Bale, Martin T., and Min-jung Ko. 2006. "Craft Production and Social Change in Mumun Pottery Period Korea." *Asian Perspectives* 45 (2): 159–87.

Barnes, Gina. 2001. *State Formation in Korea: Historical and Archaeological Perspectives*. Richmond: Curzon.

Barnes, Gina L. 2015. *Archaeology of East Asia: The Rise of Civilization in China, Korea and Japan*. Philadelphia, PA: Oxbow Books.

Baxter, Mike J., and Caitlin E. Buck. 2000. "Data Handling and Statistical Analysis." In *Modern Analytical Methods in Art and Archaeology*, edited by Enrico Ciliberto and Giuseppe Spoto, 681–746. New York: Wiley.

Baxter, Mike J., and I. C. Freestone. 2006. "Log-Ratio Compositional Data Analysis in Archaeometry." *Archaeometry* 48 (3): 511–31.

Best, Jonathan W. 1982. "Diplomatic and Cultural Contacts between Paekche and China." *Harvard Journal of Asiatic Studies* 42 (2): 443–501.

———. 2006. *A History of the Early Korean Kingdom of Paekche: Together with an Annotated Translation of the Paekche Annals of the Samguk Sagi*. Cambridge, MA: Harvard University Asia Center: Distributed by Harvard University Press.

Bieber, A. M., D. W. Brooks, G. Harbottle, and E. V. Sayre. 1976. "Application of Multivariate Techniques to Analytical Data on Aegean Ceramics." *Archaeometry* 18 (1): 59–74.

Bishop, R. L., and M. J. Blackman. 2002. "Instrumental Neutron Activation Analysis of Archaeological Ceramics: Scale and Interpretation." *Accounts of Chemical Research* 35 (8): 603–10.

Blackmore, Hari. 2019. "A Critical Examination of Models Regarding a Han 韓—Ye 濊 Ethnic Division in Proto-Historic Central Korea, and Further Implications." *Asian Perspectives* 58 (1): 95–122.

Blanton, Richard E., and Lane F. Fargher. 2008. *Collective Action in the Formation of Pre-Modern States*. Fundamental Issues in Archaeology. New York: Springer.

———. 2011. "The Collective Logic of Pre-Modern Cities." *World Archaeology* 43 (3): 505–22.

———. 2016. *How Humans Cooperate: Confronting the Challenges of Collective Action*. Boulder: University Press of Colorado.

Brumfiel, Elizabeth M., and Timothy K. Earle. 1987. *Specialization, Exchange, and Complex Societies*. Cambridge: Cambridge University Press.

Byington, Mark E., ed. 2009. *The Samhan Period in Korean History*. Cambridge, MA: Korea Institute, Harvard University.

Byington, Mark E., ed. 2012. *The Rediscovery of Kaya in History and Archaeology*. Cambridge, MA: Korea Institute, Harvard University.

———., ed. 2013. *The Han Commanderies in Early Korean History*. Early Korea Project Occasional Series. Cambridge, MA: Early Korea Project, Korea Institute, Harvard University.

Carballo, David M., and Gary M. Feinman. 2016. "Cooperation, Collective Action, and the Archeology of Large-Scale Societies." *Evolutionary Anthropology: Issues, News, and Reviews* 25 (6): 288–96.

Chilton, Elizabeth S. 1999. "One Size Fits All: Typology and Alternatives for Ceramic Research." In *Material Meanings*, edited by Elizabeth S. Chilton, 44–60. Salt Lake City: University of Utah Press.

Cho, Daeyoun. 2006. "Crafting the State: Analytical Approaches to Ceramic Technology and Exchange from the Bronze Age to Paekche Periods in Korea." PhD dissertation. Sheffield: University of Sheffield.

Choi, Jongtaik. 2008. "The Development of the Pottery Technologies of the Korean Peninsula and Their Relationship to Neighboring Regions." In *Reconsidering Early Korean History through Archaeology*, 1:157–98. Early Korea. Cambridge: Harvard University Press.

Chough, Sung Kwun. 2013. *Geology and Sedimentology of the Korean Peninsula*. New York: Elsevier.

Chough, Sung Kwun, Hee Jun Lee, and Seok Hoon Yoon. 2000. *Marine Geology of Korean Seas*. New York: Elsevier.

Clark, John E. 1995. "Craft Specialization as an Archaeological Category." *Research in Economic Anthropology* 16: 267–94.

Cogswell, J. W., H. Neff, and M. D. Glascock. 1996. "The Effect of Firing Temperature on the Elemental Characterization of Pottery." *Journal of Archaeological Science* 23 (2): 283–87.

Costin, Cathy Lynne. 1991. "Craft Specialization: Issues in Defining, Documenting, and Explaining the Organization of Production." *Archaeological Method and Theory* 3: 1–56.

———. 1998. "Introduction: Craft and Social Identity." In *Craft and Social Identity*, edited by Cathy Lynne Costin and Rita P. Wright, 3–16. Arlington, VA: American Anthropological Association.

———. 2001. "Craft Production Systems." In *Archaeology at the Millennium*, edited by Gary M. Feinman and T. Douglas Price, 273–327. New York: Kluwer Academic/Plenum.

———. 2007. "Thinking about Production: Phenomenological Classification and Lexical Semantics." In *Rethinking Craft Specialization in Complex Societies*, edited by Zachary X. Hruby and Rowan K. Flad, 143–62. Arlington, VA: American Anthropological Association.

Crumley, Carole L. 1976. "Toward a Locational Definition of State Systems of Settlement." *American Anthropologist*, New Series 78 (1): 59–73.

———. 1995. "Heterarchy and the Analysis of Complex Societies." In *Heterarchy and the Analysis of Complex Societies*, edited by Robert M. Ehrenreich, Carole L. Crumley, and Janet E. Levy, 1–5. Arlington, VA: American Anthropological Association.

———. 2005. "Remember How to Organize: Heterarchy across Disciplines." In *Nonlinear Models for Archaeology and Anthropology*, edited by Christopher Stockard Beekman and William W. Baden, 35–50. Burlington, VT: Ashgate.

———. 2007. "Notes on a New Paradigm." In *Socialising Complexity*, edited by Stephanie Wynne-Jones and Sheila Kohring, 30–36. Oxford: Oxbow Books.

Davey, Jack. 2019. "Culture Contact and Cultural Boundaries in Iron Age Southern Korea." *Asian Perspectives* 58 (1): 123–48.

Davey, Jack, and Dennis Lee. 2019. "Early Korea: Re-Thinking Boundaries and Identities." *Asian Perspectives* 58 (1): 2–6.

DeMarrais, Elizabeth. 2007. "Settings and Symbols: Assessing Complexity in the Pre-Hispanic Andes." In *Socialising Complexity*, edited by Stephanie Wynne-Jones and Sheila Kohring, 118–39. Oxford: Oxbow Books.

DeMarrais, Elizabeth, Luis Jaime Castillo, and Timothy Earle. 1996. "Ideology, Materialization, and Power Strategies." *Current Anthropology* 37 (1): 15–31.

Dobres, Marica-Anne. 1999. "Of Paradigms and Ways of Seeing: Artifact Variability as If People Mattered." In *Material Meanings*, edited by Elizabeth S. Chilton, 7–23. Salt Lake City: University of Utah Press.

Drennan, Robert. 1991. "Pre-Hispanic Chiefdom Trajectories in Mesoamerica, Central America, and Northern South America." In *Chiefdoms: Power, Economy, and Ideology*, edited by Timothy Earle, 263–87. Cambridge: Cambridge University Press.

Dueppen, Stephen A. 2012. "From Kin to Great House: Inequality and Communalism at Iron Age Kirikongo, Burkina Faso." *American Antiquity* 77 (1): 3–39.

———. 2015. "Expressing Difference: Inequality and House-Based Potting in a First-Millennium AD Community (Burkina Faso, West Africa)." *Cambridge Archaeological Journal* 25 (1): 17–43.

Earle, Timothy. 1991. *Chiefdoms: Power, Economy, and Ideology*. New York: Cambridge University Press.

Emeleus, V. M., and G. Simpson. 1960. "Neutron Activation Analysis of Ancient Roman Potsherds." *Nature* 185 (4707): 196.

Feinman, Gary, and Joyce Marcus, eds. 1998. *Archaic States*. Santa Fe, NM: School of American Research Press.

Ferguson, Yale. 1991. "Chiefdoms to City-States: The Greek Experience." In *Chiefdoms: Power, Economy, and Ideology*, edited by Timothy Earle, 169–92. Cambridge: Cambridge University Press.

Flad, Rowan K., and Zachary X. Hruby. 2007. " 'Specialized' Production in Archaeological Contexts: Rethinking Specialization, the Social Value of Products, and the Practice of Production." In *Rethinking Craft Specialization in Complex Societies*, edited by

Zachary X. Hruby and Rowan K. Flad, 1–19. Arlington, VA: American Anthropological Association.

Flannery, Kent V. 1972. "The Cultural Evolution of Civilizations." *Annual Review of Ecology and Systematics* 3: 399–426.

Frachetti, Michael D. 2012. "Multiregional Emergence of Mobile Pastoralism and Nonuniform Institutional Complexity across Eurasia." *Current Anthropology* 53 (1): 2–38. doi:10.1086/663692.

Fried, Morton. 1967. *The Evolution of Political Society: An Essay in Political Anthropology*. New York: Random House.

Gilman, Antonio. 1991. "Trajectories towards Social Complexity in the Later Prehistory of the Mediterranean." In *Chiefdoms: Power, Economy, and Ideology*, edited by Timothy Earle, 146–68. Cambridge: Cambridge University Press.

Glascock, Michael D., and Hector Neff. 2003. "Neutron Activation Analysis and Provenance Research in Archaeology." *Measurement Science and Technology* 14 (9): 1516–1526.

Glascock, M. D., H. Neff, and K. J. Vaughn. 2004. "Instrumental Neutron Activation Analysis and Multivariate Statistics for Pottery Provenance." *Hyperfine Interactions* 154 (1–4): 95–105.

Gopnik, Hilary, Clemens Reichel, Leah Minc, and Rasha Elendari. June 2016. "A View from the East: The Godin VI Oval and the Uruk Sphere." *Journal of Archaeological Science: Reports* 7: 835–48.

Gosselain, Olivier P. 1998. "Social and Technical Identity in a Clay Crystal Ball." In *The Archaeology of Social Boundaries*, edited by Miriam T. Stark, 78–106. Washington, DC: Smithsonian Institution Press.

———. 2000. "Materializing Identities: An African Perspective." *Journal of Archaeological Method and Theory* 7 (3): 187–217.

———. 2016. "To Hell with Ethnoarchaeology!" *Archaeological Dialogues* 23 (2): 215–28.

Grave, P., M. Stark, D. Ea, L. Kealhofer, B. S. Tan, and T. Tin. 2017. "Differentiating Khmer Stoneware Production: An NAA Pilot Study from Siem Reap Province, Cambodia." *Archaeometry* 59 (1): 13–24.

Habu, Junko, Clare Fawcett, and John M. Matsunaga, eds. 2008. *Evaluating Multiple Narratives: Beyond Nationalist, Colonialist, Imperialist Archaeologies.* New York: Springer.

Hangang Institute of Cultural Heritage (HICH). 2008. *Donghwa-Ri Site, Wonju.* Research Report 1. Seoul: Hangang Institute of Cultural Heritage. In Korean.

———. 2012a. *Jungsanidong Site, Incheon.* Research Report 20. Seoul: Hangang Institute of Cultural Heritage. In Korean.

———. 2012b. *Unbuk-dong Site, Incheon.* Research Report 24. Seoul: Hangang Institute of Cultural Heritage. In Korean.

———. 2013. *Bangok-dong Site, Wonju.* Research Report 37. Bucheon: Hangang Institute of Cultural Heritage. In Korean.

Hannam University Central Museum (HUCM). 2006. *Pottery Kiln Sites at Samryong-ri and Sansu-ri, Jincheon-gun.* Archaeological Research Report 24. Daejeon: Hannam University Press. In Korean.

Hanshin University Museum (HUM). 2006. *Pungnap Earthen Wall VII.* Hanshin University Museum Research Series 24. Osan: Hanshin University Press. In Korean.

Harbottle, Garman. 1982. "Provenience Studies Using Neutron Activation Analysis: The Role of Standardization." In *Archaeological Ceramics*, edited by Jacqueline S. Olin and Alan D. Franklin, 67–77. Washington, DC: Smithsonian Institution Press.

Hayden, Brian. 1998. "Practical and Prestige Technologies: The Evolution of Material Systems." *Journal of Archaeological Method and Theory* 5 (1): 1–55.

Helms, Mary W. 1993. *Craft and the Kingly Ideal.* Austin: University of Texas Press.

Hirshman, Amy J., William A. Lovis, and Helen P. Pollard. 2010. "Specialization of Ceramic Production: A Sherd Assemblage Based Analytic Perspective." *Journal of Anthropological Archaeology* 29 (3): 265–77.

Hirth, Kenneth G. 1996. "Political Economy and Archaeology: Perspectives on Exchange and Production." *Journal of Archaeological Research* 4 (3): 203–39.

Honeychurch, William. 2013. "The Nomad as State Builder: Historical Theory and Material Evidence from Mongolia." *Journal of World Prehistory* 26 (4): 283–321.

———. 2014. "Alternative Complexities: The Archaeology of Pastoral Nomadic States." *Journal of Archaeological Research* 22 (4): 277–326.

Ju, Bo Don. 2009. "Problems Concerning the Basic Historical Documents Related to the Samhan." In *The Samhan Period in Korean History*. Vol. 2. Early Korea. Cambridge: Harvard University Press.

Jung, In-seung. 2013. "The Material Culture of Lelang Commandery." In *The Han Commanderies in Early Korean History*, edited by Mark E. Byington, 137–64. Early Korea Project Occasional Series. Cambridge, MA: Harvard University Press.

Junker, Laura Lee. 1999. *Raiding, Trading, and Feasting: The Political Economy of Philippine Chiefdoms*. Honolulu: University of Hawaii Press.

Kabata-Pendias, Alina, and Arun B. Mukherjee. 2007. *Trace Elements from Soil to Human*. New York: Springer.

Kidder, J. Edward. 2007. *Himiko and Japan's Elusive Chiefdom of Yamatai: Archaeology, History, and Mythology*. Honolulu: University of Hawaii Press.

Kim, Jangsuk. 2014. "The Appearance of Lattice Pattern Pottery and U-Shaped Pottery in Central Korea (중부지역 격자문타날토기와 U자형토기의 등장)." *Korean Archaeology (한국고고학보)* 90: 76–119. In Korean.

Kim, Minkoo, Heung-Nam Shin, Jinhee Kim, Kyeong-jung Roh, Ara Ryu, Haesun Won, Juho Kim, Semi Oh, Hyeongsin Noh, and Sumin Kim. September 2016. "The Ins and the Outs: Foodways, Feasts, and Social Differentiation in the Baekje Kingdom, Korea." *Journal of Anthropological Archaeology* 43: 128–39.

Kim, Seung-Og. 2014. "Structure and Characteristics of Jeonnam Region's Mahan Society through an Analysis of settlements (전남지역 마한 제국의 사회 성격과 백제; 취락으로 본 전남지역 마한 사회의 구조와 성격)." *Baekje Communications (백제학보)* 11: 33–72. In Korean.

———. 2015. "Recent Developments and Debates in Korean Prehistoric Archaeology." *Asian Perspectives* 54 (1): 11–30.

Kirch, Patrick. 1991. "Chiefship and Competitive Involution: The Marquesas Islands of Eastern Polynesia." In *Chiefdoms: Power, Economy, and Ideology*, edited by Timothy Earle, 119–45. Cambridge: Cambridge University Press.

Kohring, Sheila, Carlos P. Odriozola, and Victor M. Hurtado. 2007. "Materializing 'Complex' Relationships: Technology Production and Consumption in a Copper Age Community." In *Socialising Complexity*, edited by Stephanie Wynne-Jones and Sheila Kohring, 100–17. Oxford: Oxbow Books.

Korean Institute of Geoscience and Mineral Resources (KIGAM). 2017. "Geological Map: 50,000:1." Accessed June 12, 2017. https://mgeo.kigam.re.kr/.

Kristiansen, Kristian. 1991. "Chiefdoms, States, and Systems of Social Evolution." In *Chiefdoms: Power, Economy, and Ideology*, edited by Timothy Earle, 16–43. Cambridge: Cambridge University Press.

———. 2007. "The Rules of the Game: Decentralized Complexity and Power." In *Socialising Complexity*, edited by Stephanie Wynne-Jones and Sheila Kohring, 60–75. Oxford: Oxbow Books.

Kwon, Oh Young. 2008. "The Influence of Recent Archaeological Discoveries on the Research of Paekche History." In *Reconsidering Early Korean History through Archaeology*. Vol. 1. Early Korea. Cambridge: Harvard University Press.

Lechtman, Heather. 1977. "Style in Technology: Some Early Thoughts." In *Material Culture*, edited by Heather Lechtman and Robert S. Merrill, 3–20. St. Paul: West.

Lee, Dennis. 2014. "Keyhole-Shaped Tombs and Unspoken Frontiers: Exploring the Borderlands of Early Korean-Japanese Relations in the 5th–6th Centuries." PhD dissertation. Los Angeles: University of California Los Angeles.

Lee, DoHack. 2013. "A Transition of Mahan Many States in Yeongsan River Basin and Baekje (영산강유역 마한제국의 추이와 백제)." *Baekje Culture (백제문화)* 49: 109–28. In Korean.

Lee, Gyoung-Ah. October 2011. "The Transition from Foraging to Farming in Prehistoric Korea." *Current Anthropology* 52: S307–29.

Lee, Jaehyun. 2009. "The Interregional Relationships and Developmental Processes of Samhan Culture." In *The Samhan Period in Korean History*. Vol. 2. Early Korea. Cambridge: Harvard University Press.

Lee, Nam-Seok. 2013. "Understanding Mahan's Tombs and Its Burial System (마한분묘와 그 묘제의 인식)." *Mahan and Baekje Culture (마한백제문화)* 22: 115–43. In Korean.

Lee, Sungsi. 2013. "The Samhan, Ye, and Wa in the Time of the Lelang and Daifang Commanderies." In *The Han Commanderies in Early Korean History*, edited by Mark E. Byington, 165–89. Cambridge, MA: Harvard University Press.

Lee, Young Cheol. 2011. "Settlement Change of the Upper Region of Youngsan River and the Transformation of Being Baekje (영산강 상류지역의 취락변동과 백제화 과정)." *Baekje Communications (백제학보)* 6: 107–40. In Korean.

Lemonnier, Pierre. 1992. *Elements for an Anthropology of Technology*. Ann Arbor, MI: Museum of Anthropology, University of Michigan.

———. 1993. "Introduction." In *Technological Choices: Transformation in Material Cultures since the Neolithic*, edited by Pierre Lemonnier, 1–35. New York: Routledge.

Levy, Janet E. 1995. "Heterarchy in Bronze Age Denmark: Settlement Pattern, Gender, Ritual." In *Heterarchy and the Analysis of Complex Societies*, edited by Robert M. Ehrenreich, Carole L. Crumley, and Janet E. Levy, 41–54. Arlington, VA: American Anthropological Association.

Lindsay, Ian, Leah Minc, Christophe Descantes, Robert J. Speakman, and Michael D. Glascock. 2008. "Exchange Patterns, Boundary Formation, and Sociopolitical Change in Late Bronze Age Southern Caucasia: Preliminary Results from a Pottery Provenance Study in Northwestern Armenia." *Journal of Archaeological Science* 35 (6): 1673–82.

Livingstone, David. 2009. *A Practical Guide to Scientific Data Analysis*. Chichester, UK: Wiley.

Michelaki, Kostalena, Gregory V. Braun, and Ronald G. V. Hancock. 2015. "Local Clay Sources as Histories of Human-Landscape Interactions: A Ceramic Taskscape Perspective." *Journal of Archaeological Method and Theory* 22 (3): 783–827.

Michelaki, Kostalena, and Ronald G. V. Hancock. 2011. "Chemistry versus Data Dispersion: Is There a Better Way to Assess and Interpret Archaeometric Data?" *Archaeometry* 53 (6): 1259–79.

Michelaki, Kostalena, Ronald G. V. Hancock, and Gregory V. Braun. 2012. "Using Provenance Data to Assess Archaeological Landscapes: An Example from Calabria, Italy." *Journal of Archaeological Science* 39 (2): 234–46.

Minc, Leah D. 2006. "Monitoring Regional Market Systems in Prehistory: Models, Methods, and Metrics." *Journal of Anthropological Archaeology* 25 (1): 82–116.

———. 2009. "Style and Substance: Evidence for Regionalism within the Aztec Market System." *Latin American Antiquity* 20 (2): 343–74.

Minc, Leah D., and Johannes H. Sterba. 2017. "Instrumental Neutron Activation Analysis (INAA) in the Study of Archaeological Ceramics." In *The Oxford Handbook of Archaeological Ceramic Analysis*, edited by Alice M. W. Hunt, 424–46. Oxford: Oxford University Press.

Monroe, J. Cameron. 2010. "Power by Design: Architecture and Politics in Precolonial Dahomey." *Journal of Social Archaeology* 10 (3): 367–97.

———. 2013. "Power and Agency in Precolonial African States." *Annual Review of Anthropology* 42 (1): 17–35.

Moon, An-sik. 2014. "The Process of Incorporating the Jeonnam Areas of Baekje into the Mahan states (전남지역 마한 제국의 사회 성격과 백제; 백제의 전남지역 마한 제국 편입 과정 – 서남해지역 및 연안도서를 중심으로)." *Baekje Communications* (백제학보) 11: 111–38. In Korean.

Nam, Sangwon. 2013. "As Production Technology, the Meaning of the Black Burnished Pottery in Baekje Dynasty (제작 기술을 통해 본 백제 흑색마연토기의 의미)." *Korean Archaeology (한국고고학보)* 89: 94–137. In Korean.

Nam, Sangwon, Rory Walsh, and Gyoung-Ah Lee. September 2020. "Innovation, Imitation, and Identity: Mayeon Black Ware and Social Complexity in Southwestern Korea." *Archaeological Research in Asia* 23: 100197.

Neff, Hector. 2000. "Neutron Activation Analysis for Provenance Determination in Archaeology." In *Modern Analytical Methods in Art and Archaeology*, edited by Enrico Ciliberto and Giuseppe Spoto, 81–134. New York: Wiley.

Nelson, Sarah. 1993. *The Archaeology of Korea*. Cambridge: Cambridge University Press.

Oh, Youngchan. 2013. "The Ruling Class of Lelang Commandery." In *The Han Commanderies in Early Korean History*, edited by Mark E Byington, 101–35. Early Korea Project Occasional Series. Cambridge, MA: Harvard University Press.

O'Reilly, Dougald J. W. 2000. "From the Bronze Age to the Iron Age in Thailand: Applying the Heterarchical Approach." *Asian Perspectives* 39 (1): 1–19.

Orton, Clive, and Mike Hughes. 2013. *Pottery in Archaeology*. Cambridge: Cambridge University Press.

Pai, Hyung Il. 2000. *Constructing "Korean" Origins: A Critical Review of Archaeology, Historiography, and Racial Myth in Korean State-Formation Theories*. Cambridge, MA: Harvard University Asia Center.

Pailes, Matthew C. 2016. "Exchange Economies of Late Prehistoric Eastern Sonora, Mexico: A Re-Evaluation Based on Provenance Data Analyses." *Journal of Field Archaeology* 41 (5): 587–602.

Park, Jungkyun. 2015. "A Study on the Conversion into Baekje from Mahan and Existence Aspects of Local Power in the Miho River Basin (미호천유역의 마한에서 백제로의 전환과 재지세력의 존재양태)." *Hoseo Archaeology (호서고고학)* 30: 70–103. In Korean.

Parkinson, William A., and Michael L. Galaty. 2007. "Secondary States in Perspective: An Integrated Approach to State Formation in the Prehistoric Aegean." *American Anthropologist* 109 (1): 113–29.

Pauketat, Timothy. 2007. *Chiefdoms and Other Archaeological Delusions*. Lanham, MD: AltaMira Press.

Peregrine, Peter. 1991. "Some Political Aspects of Craft Specialization." *World Archaeology* 23 (1): 1–11.

Perlman, I., and F. Asaro. 1969. "Pottery Analysis by Neutron Activation." *Archaeometry* 11 (1): 21–38.

Pollard, A. Mark, Carl Heron, and Ruth Ann Armitage. 2017. *Archaeological Chemistry*. 3rd ed. Cambridge: Royal Society of Chemistry.

Reedy, Chandra L. 2008. *Thin-Section Petrography of Stone and Ceramic Cultural Materials*. London: Archetype.

Rhee, Song Nai. 1992. "Secondary State Formation: The Case of the Koguryo State." In *Pacific Northeast Asia in Prehistory*, edited by C. Melvin Aikens and Song Nai Rhee, 191–96. Pullman, WA: WSU Press.

Rhee, Song Nai, C. Melvin Aikens, Sŏng-nak Ch'oe, and Hyŏk-chin No. 2007. "Korean Contributions to Agriculture, Technology, and State Formation in Japan: Archaeology and History of an Epochal Thousand Years, 400 B.C.–A.D. 600." *Asian Perspectives* 46 (2): 404–59.

Rhee, Song Nai, and Mong-Lyong Choi. 1992. "Emergence of Complex Society in Prehistoric Korea." *Journal of World Prehistory* 6 (1): 51–95.

Rice, Prudence M. 2017. *Pottery Analysis: A Sourcebook*. 2nd ed. Chicago, IL: University of Chicago Press.

Rogers, J. Daniel. 2007. "The Contingencies of State Formation in Eastern Inner Asia." *Asian Perspectives* 46 (2): 249–74.

Rollinson, Hugh R. 2014. *Using Geochemical Data: Evaluation, Presentation, Interpretation*. New York: Routledge.

Roux, V. 2003. "Ceramic Standardization and Intensity of Production: Quantifying Degrees of Specialization." *American Antiquity* 68 (4): 768–82.

Sayre, E. V., R. W. Dodson, and Dorothy Burr Thompson. 1957. "Neutron Activation Study of Mediterranean Potsherds." *American Journal of Archaeology* 61 (1): 35–41.

Schortman, Edward M., and Patricia A. Urban. 2004. "Modeling the Roles of Craft Production in Ancient Political Economies." *Journal of Archaeological Research* 12 (2): 185–226.

Seo, Hyun-ju. 2014. "A Study on the Character of Mahan Society in the Jeonnam Region through the Excavated Artifacts: With a Focus on the Earthenware from the 5th and 6th Century (전남지역 마한 제국의 사회 성격과 백제; 출토유물로 본 전남지역 마한제국의 사회 성격 -5~6세기 토기를 중심으로)." *Baekje Communications* (백제학보) 11: 71–90. In Korean.

Seong, JeongYong. 2012. "Aspects and Nature of Pottery from Iseong Fortress, Jeungpyeng (증평 이성산성 출토 토기양상과 그 성격." *Hoseo Archaeology* (호서고고학) 27: 44–65. In Korean.

———. 2016. "Results of the 2015 Archaeological Investigations of the Mahan and Baekje Relics in the Hoseo Region (호서지역의 마한과 백제 유적조사 성과)." *Baekje Communications* (백제학보) 18: 5–33. In Korean.

Seoul Baekje Museum and Hanshin University Museum (SBM-HUM). 2011. *Pungnap Earthen Wall XII: Excavation Report of the Site No. 196 at Gyeongdang District*. Hanshin University Museum Research Series 37. Osan: Hanshin University Press. In Korean.

———. 2015. *Pungnap Earthen Wall XVII: Excavation Report of the Site No. 206 at Gyeongdang District*. Hanshin University Museum Research Series 41. Osan: Hanshin University Press. In Korean.

Service, Elman. 1971. *Primitive Social Organization: An Evolutionary Perspective*. 2nd ed. New York: Random House.

Shelach, Gideon, and Yitzhak Jaffe. 2014. "The Earliest States in China: A Long-Term Trajectory Approach." *Journal of Archaeological Research* 22 (4): 327–64.

Shelach, Gideon, and Yuri Pines. 2006. "Secondary State Formation and the Development of Local Identity: Change and Continuity in the State of Qin (770–221 B.C.)." In *Archaeology of Asia*, edited by Miriam T. Stark, 202–30. Malden, MA: Blackwell.

Smith, Michael E. 2004. "The Archaeology of Ancient State Economies." *Annual Review of Anthropology* 33: 73–102.

Sneath, David. 2007. "The Decentralized State: Nomads, Complexity, and Sociotechnical Systems in Inner Asia." In *Socialising Complexity*, edited by Stephanie Wynne-Jones and Sheila Kohring, 228–44. Oxford: Oxbow Books.

Stahl, Ann B., Maria das Dores Cruz, Hector Neff, Michael D. Glascock, Robert J. Speakman, Bretton Giles, and Leith Smith. 2008. "Ceramic Production, Consumption and Exchange in the Banda Area, Ghana: Insights from Compositional Analyses." *Journal of Anthropological Archaeology* 27 (3): 363–81.

Stark, Miriam T. 1998. "Technical Choices and Social Boundaries in Material Culture Patterning: An Introduction." In *The Archaeology of Social Boundaries*, edited by Miriam T. Stark, 1–11. Washington, DC: Smithsonian Institution Press.

Stark, Miriam T., R. L. Bishop, and E. Miksa. 2000. "Ceramic Technology and Social Boundaries: Cultural Practices in Kalinga Clay Selection and Use." *Journal of Archaeological Method and Theory* 7 (4): 295–331.

Steponaitis, Vincas. 1991. "Contrasting Patterns of Mississippian Development." In *Chiefdoms: Power, Economy, and Ideology*, edited by Timothy Earle, 193–228. Cambridge: Cambridge University Press.

Stimmell, Carole, Robert B. Heimann, and Ronald G. V. Hancock. 1982. "Indian Pottery from the Mississippi Valley: Coping with Bad Raw Materials." In *Archaeological Ceramics*, edited by Jacqueline S. Olin and Alan D. Franklin, 219–43. Washington, DC: Smithsonian Institution Press.

Tsushida, Junko. 2013. "Development of Cookery Tools Excavated in Mahan and Baekje Areas (일반논문: 마한, 백제지역 취사용기 변천고)." *Baekje Research* (백제연구) 58: 151–81. In Korean.

Underhill, Anne P. 2003. "Investigating Variation in Organization of Ceramic Production: An Ethnoarchaeological Study in Guizhou, China." *Journal of Archaeological Method and Theory* 10 (3): 203–75.

Underhill, Anne P. 2015. "What Is Special about Specialization?" In *Emerging Trends in the Social and Behavioral Sciences*, edited by R.A. Scott and S.M. Kosslyn. New York: John Wiley & Sons. doi: 10.1002/9781118900772.etrds0384

van der Leeuw, Sander. 1993. "Giving the Potter a Choice: Conceptual Aspects of Pottery Techniques." In *Technological Choices*, edited by Pierre Lemonnier, 238–88. London: Routledge.

Vaughn, Kevin J. 2006. "Craft Production, Exchange, and Political Power in the Pre-Incaic Andes." *Journal of Archaeological Research* 14 (4): 313–44.

Walsh, Rory. 2017. "Ceramic Specialization and Exchange in Complex Societies: A Compositional Analysis of Pottery from Mahan and Baekje in Southwestern Korea." PhD dissertation, Eugene: University of Oregon.

White, Joyce C. 1995. "Incorporating Heterarchy into Theory on Socio-Political Development: The Case for Southeast Asia." In *Heterarchy and the Analysis of Complex Societies*, edited by Robert M. Ehrenreich, Carole L. Crumley, and Janet E. Levy, 101–24. Arlington, VA: American Anthropological Association.

Wright, Henry T., and Gregory A. Johnson. 1975. "Population, Exchange, and Early State Formation in Southwestern Iran." *American Anthropologist*, New Series 77 (2): 267–89.

Wynne-Jones, Stephanie. 2007. "Multiple Landscapes and Layered Meanings: Scale, Interaction and Process in the Development of a Swahili Town." In *Socialising Complexity*, edited by Stephanie Wynne-Jones and Sheila Kohring, 142–60. Oxford: Oxbow Books.

Wynne-Jones, Stephanie, and Sheila Kohring. 2007. "Socialising Complexity." In *Socialising Complexity*, edited by Stephanie Wynne-Jones and Sheila Kohring, 2–12. Oxford: Oxbow Books.

Yang, Gi-seok. 2013. "Mahan and Baekje in South Jeolla Province (전남지역 마한 소국과 백제: 전남지역 마한사회와 백제)." *Baekje Communications* (백제학보) 9: 1–21. In Korean.

Yao, Alice. 2010. "Recent Developments in the Archaeology of Southwestern China." *Journal of Archaeological Research* 18 (3): 203–39.

———. 2012. "Sarmatian Mirrors and Han Ingots (100 BC–AD 100): How the Foreign Became Local and Vice Versa." *Cambridge Archaeological Journal* 22 (1): 57–70.

Yi, Hyunhae. 2009. "The Formation and Development of the Samhan." In *The Samhan Period in Korean History*. Vol. 2. Early Korea. Cambridge: Harvard University Press.

Yim, Young-jin. 2014. "Social Characteristics of the Mahan State-lets in the Jeonnam Region and Their Relationship with Baekje (전남지역 마한 제국의 사회 성격과 백제; 전남지역 마한 제국의 사회 성격과 백제)." *Baekje Communications (백제학보)* 11: 5–32. In Korean.

Zagarell, Allen. 1995. "Hierarchy and Heterarchy: The Unity of Opposites." In *Heterarchy and the Analysis of Complex Societies*, edited by Robert M. Ehrenreich, Carole L. Crumley, and Janet E. Levy, 87–100. Arlington, VA: American Anthropological Association.

Zeder, Melinda. 1991. *Feeding Cities: Specialized Animal Economy in the Ancient Near East*. Washington, DC: Smithsonian Institution Press.